48

The Christian
Working Woman

The Christian Working Woman

What You Need to Know

Mary Whelchel

Fleming H. Revell

A Division of Baker Book House Co
Grand Rapids, Michigan 49516

Published by Fleming H. Revell
a division of Baker Book House Company
P.O. Box 6287, Grand Rapids, MI 49516-6287

Paperback edition published 1998

Printed in the United States of America

Library of Congress Cataloging-in-Publication Data

Whelchel, Mary.
    The Christian working woman : what you need to know / Mary
Whelchel.—Pbk. ed.
       p.   cm.
    Originally published: 1994.
    ISBN 0-8007-5537-5 (pbk.)
    1. Christian women—Conduct of life. 2. Christian women—
Employment. I. Title.
    [BJ1610.W52   1998]
    248.8'43—dc21
                                                 97-42355

For current information about all releases from Baker Book House, visit our web site:
http://www.bakerbooks.com

To my mother

My role model for Christian womanhood,
whose walk with God continually challenges me,
whose friendship constantly encourages me,
whose prayers faithfully support me,
and whose love quietly affirms me

Contents

Preface

I wrote this book for one reason: to encourage and challenge Christian women who, for whatever reason, are a part of the working world outside their homes. I am one of those women and have been for more than twenty years. So I write as an insider—one who has made about every mistake you can imagine and who still struggles with many issues. Now, eight years since the first edition, I write as one who has had constant and increasing contact with these women through my radio program, "The Christian Working Woman," now heard on more than three hundred stations across the country, and through my many speaking engagements. That gives me a great advantage in writing a book like this, because I probably have more input and contact with Christian women in the workplace from every state, every career, every status level, and every kind of experience than anyone else. I am privileged to be in that position.

This book needed updating because times have changed and I have changed as God has given me many opportunities for growth in these past few years. I said in the preface to the first edition that I didn't have all the answers, and I realize more than ever how true that is. But thankfully, God does not require perfection of us as a prerequisite to service. We don't have to have all our act together in order to be of use to him. He chooses to use us while we're right in the middle of learning and growing and putting the pieces together. Only a truly powerful and magnificent God could pull that off!

I began my ministry for workplace women to fill what I saw as an obvious need in churches and in Christian ministry. While things have improved somewhat in the last eight years, still there is little support or encouragement for working women in most Christian environments. These women still often feel quite guilty for entering the working world, even when they have no real option.

I hope this book will continue that gap-filling purpose. I pray that, tucked in among these many words, there are some insights that will give direction and hope to Christian working women. I am totally convinced that God's Word is relevant to every issue we face, regardless of our circumstances.

Knowing how to apply biblical principles, though, is not always clear to us. As I've faced various situations and talked with other women about their particular problems, I've searched for "handles" to put on the truth of God. I need simple, practical ideas and approaches that help me take the words off the pages of the Bible and make them reality in my everyday life.

This book, then, is a compilation of some of those ideas that God has given to me to help me apply his principles to my life as a working woman. I believe the topics discussed are ones that most working women face at one point or another. I have tried to write openly and candidly, as though I were speaking to you directly. I would like to think that by the time you finish reading this, we will be good friends. Mostly, I hope something I've written will help you.

Full-Time Job—
Part-Time Christian?

Let me ask you a two-part question: Why do you work, and why do you have the particular job you have? Some of you would undoubtedly answer that you work simply because you have to—to put bread on the table. So many workplace women are there because they are the sole support for themselves and often for their children as well. Perhaps you would say that you work because you really enjoy the challenge and have career ambitions that interest you. Or maybe you're working to supplement the family income or to pay for a college education for your child. Maybe you work just to get out of the house. There would be, I'm sure, quite a variety of answers to this question.

My own answers have changed greatly over the years of my career. I entered the working world out of necessity. Becoming a businesswoman had never been my dream or plan. I pursued a career because I had to earn a living for my daughter and myself. I certainly got caught up in advancing my career, and I frequently enjoyed the challenge and rewards of my work. But essentially I was working because I had to. Only in the last half of my career have I begun to see my job as having any eternal significance.

What I discovered about myself—and what I find true about many Christians in the working world—is that we tend to mentally divide our lives into two parts. Our jobs and the other mundane activities of our lives we tend to classify as secular, and our church activities and whatever other ministries we may have are considered sacred. And because our jobs demand so much of our time, the secular department is considerably larger than the sacred department. These designations are not usually conscious ones, but they exist nonetheless in our thinking.

Furthermore, we tend to view our being working people out in the everyday business world in a different light than people who choose some public ministry for their life's work. There is an underlying attitude that these people in public ministries are of more service to God than those of us who are in the working world. We say that people who are in public ministries in a church or Christian organization are in full-time Christian service. Somehow, we tend to think that the organization from which we get our paycheck determines whether we're in full-time Christian service or not.

Men and women in public ministries are expected to talk about the Lord, to witness, to encourage people, to study God's Word, to pray a lot. But here you and I are, working at secular jobs, and our duties don't exactly lend themselves to talking about the Lord or concentrating on spiritual matters. We have to be concerned with pleasing our bosses, getting the letters typed, answering the telephone, talking with clients, taking orders, teaching our students, attending patients, tracking statistics—or whatever particular duties our job encompasses. In our minds we may fail to see any connection between these secular duties and our Christian commitment.

Well, is there any connection? When my daughter was in college I spoke to the business association at the Christian college she attended, and one of the things I emphasized with this group of Christian young adults getting ready to embark on careers in business was this: If you have committed your life to Jesus Christ, you are in full-time Christian service. God expects as much of you as he expects of preachers and missionaries. There are no sacred and secular departments with God. The same power available to people in public ministries is available to us who go to our working worlds every day.

Nowhere in Scripture do we find any mention of this idea of full-time Christian work. In fact, you'll notice that most of the people greatly used by God had what we would call secular occupations. Paul was a tentmaker, Lydia was a seller of purple, Peter, James, and John were fishermen, Deborah was the ruler of her country. So let's try to dispel this mind-set about full-time Christian service as that work done only by people who receive paychecks from Christian organizations.

Do you view your job as the place where God has you at this time for his purposes, to teach you and to use you as a light in darkness? You may say, "Well, I've never thought about it that way. I don't know if I've ever really considered whether this is where God wants me to be or not." But do you think it's less important for those of us who work in the business world to know that we're where God wants us to be than it is for our ministers or missionaries? When we get up to go to work in the morning, we should have a sense of commitment to what God has called us to do and a surety that we are headed to the place where he wants us to be, just as much as our pastors do when they go to their offices at our churches.

If you are sure of God's direction for you in the working world, then your role there is just as sacred, just as important to God, and of just as much service to him as anything else you could do. It is not second best; it is not the alternative for those who have never sensed a call into a public ministry. It is full-time Christian service!

As I mentioned earlier, for many years I thought of my job as a separate part of my life. At that point I was placing too much importance on advancing my career, and I did not view my job as God's mission for me. But now I realize that God is not inefficient. He would not have me spend such a great part of my life doing something that is not important to him. Indeed, he intends for me, and for all Christians in the working world, to see my job as his mission field for my service to him.

In John 17 Jesus prays for his disciples and says,

> I am no more in the world; and yet they themselves are in the world, and I come to Thee Holy Father, keep them in Thy name. . . . I do not ask Thee to take them out of the world, but to keep them from the evil one. They are not of the world, even as I am not of the world. . . . As Thou didst send Me into the world, I also have sent them into the world.
>
> verses 11, 15, 16, 18

Jesus said he was praying this not only for his disciples then, but for all of us who would believe in him (v. 20). That's you and me!

You know, God could have taken us to him as soon as we accepted Christ. Why not? That would have been nice for us. We would be relieved of all this grief and sin and work and sorrow—and just immediately be transported to his presence! Or he could supply every need we have so that we could all live together in separate Christian communities and not have to associate with all the evil characterizing the world today. But he has so arranged it that we have to be in the world; we have to go out and make our living in this world.

Have you ever thought of this: God has designed work as the common denominator for the Christian and non-Christian, and the job is the place where the Christian must meet the non-Christian world. This is no accident. God has planned it that way! Is it really any mystery why God would have his people out in this business world? After all, that's where the people are who need him. God can, and indeed does, purposely send us out into the working world as his witnesses, his light. Is this any less important or of lesser value to God than someone who is in Africa translating Scripture? No.

Likely, you have heard sermons that touched on this subject before. But I wonder if, like me, you have been treating your job as a necessary part of your life—something to be endured, hopefully financially rewarding, maybe even interesting—but never really looking at it as your mission in life.

Jesus said he has sent us into the world. None of us is exempted from this. Regardless of your personality or your talents or your abilities, if you are a Christian, you are sent! It's not a matter of waiting for a "call." It's not a matter of deciding whether we want to be sent or not! Christ has sent us into the world; there are no options. And where is your world into which you are sent? It includes your working world, whether that world is an office or a store or a classroom or a hospital or a factory. That is the world into which you are sent.

In answer to the question I posed at the beginning, can we not then say that our jobs are the part of the world into which God has sent us to minister? That job you have is your corner of the world where you are sent. If you don't cover it, nobody else will.

Okay, you may say, so God has sent me. So, my corner of the world is just as important as any other corner. But when I get to my corner, I can't preach or teach or witness all day. I have to work. How can that be a mission? The neat thing about being sent into the working world is that we get in on equal footing. We're not a different set—a minority—we're one of the gang. Our ministers can't get in there, as ministers, and get to know these people we work with as we do. They would be outsiders, but we're there. We have a right to be there. We have a duty to be there. And in that place where we are sent, though we cannot preach or teach or continually witness verbally, our lives can become that inescapable witness to what God can do for and with any person who is committed to him. Our fellow workers cannot ignore or deny a witness that is lived in front of their eyes.

In Matthew 5:16 Jesus said, "Let your light so shine before men, that they may see your good works, and glorify your Father which is in heaven" (KJV). How can we be lights and witnesses in the part of the world to which we are sent? First Peter 3:15 tells us to always be ready to give an answer to everyone who asks us to give an account for the hope that is in us, yet with gentleness and reverence.

Let me assure you of this: If you begin to view your job as the place in the world where God has sent you—and only you—to be his witness and his light, it won't be long before you will have an opportunity to give an account for the hope that is in you. The most effective witness is one that comes as a result of a question. And if you relate to your job as your mission from God, your behavior and your life will be different. That difference will cause people to be curious, and sooner or later they'll ask you why you are different.

But it begins with a changed attitude toward our jobs. We cannot treat our jobs as separate parts of our lives—secular rather than sacred. They must be viewed as the corner of the world into which we have been sent by Jesus. As one who is still learning this lesson herself, I want to encourage you to ask God to change your thinking about your job. It will give it a completely new importance. You'll be amazed at how much more meaningful everyday life becomes when you view your job as your mission, as indeed it is.

In the chapters that follow, we'll first take a look at ourselves, our attitudes and attributes, and how we can prepare ourselves for covering our corner of the world. Then we'll discuss some problem situations and how to use God's principles in dealing with them. We'll see that, truly, God's Word is relevant to every issue we face.

1
Multiple Roles but One Identity

Whether a woman is working to supplement the family income, to fulfill lifelong aspirations, or from necessity as a single woman or single parent, she usually finds herself playing several roles. Although multiple roles are not new, the working woman of today seems to be struggling for identity. Which of her roles is most important? In which role does she find her real self?

Feeling pressured by her own expectations, as well as those of her family, employers, and friends, she falls prey to the "Superwoman complex." She senses an unspoken demand from society to give a walk-on-water performance at all times. Trying to be all things to all people, she becomes a prime candidate for an identity crisis.

How well I remember the shock to my own identity when I began my career. I was selected as one of the first female sales reps for one of America's leading companies. And I was immersed into a very male world almost overnight—the only female rep in my office, and the first female sales rep most of my customers had ever seen. In addition, I was struggling with singleness, having recently been divorced. Since I had never planned to be a career woman, and certainly never a divorced woman, these were unfamiliar roles that were thrust on me unexpectedly.

At the time, I probably would not have verbalized my situation as an identity crisis, but indeed those new circumstances were the beginning of a long struggle for my identity. I wanted to be a very feminine female and not allow this new role of career woman to make me insensitive and aggressive, but at the same time I wanted to be successful. And I was looking for the right man to validate my femininity, to prove I was an attractive woman. In addition, my daughter was eight at the time, and I, a single parent, certainly wanted to be a first-rate mother too. I was also a Christian, and I tried to fit my Christianity into all these other roles and demands. How could I possibly make all of them come together successfully in one very human and very fallible person . . . me?

What began to happen was that the roles became very un-balanced. I was so anxious and determined to succeed in my career, and so desperate to be affirmed as a woman as well, that my whole emphasis in life shifted to those goals and objectives. Those roles took priority and the others suffered. In particular, my relationship with God really took a backseat. Though I was a Christian, I lost that unique quality that every Christian should have, that light and salt in a dark and tasteless world. I blended in with everyone else. I did not want to be different. I wanted to be a sophisticated, savvy business lady, and I wanted to attract a male counterpart. That was the focus of my life for many years.

Though my circumstances precipitated my role-juggling identity imbalance, I cannot use my career or my divorce as an excuse for my failure to have balanced priorities. It is certainly possible for Christians with varied duties to have a balanced, Christ-honoring perspective of their roles and to perform well in each without having misplaced priorities. So the many hats I wore were not the problem.

I now know it was my "evil, unbelieving heart" (Heb. 3:12) that caused the identity crisis I was experiencing. It was my own lack of understanding of who God is and how he feels about me and what his intentions are toward me. And because my comprehension of God was inaccurate and inadequate, I was afraid to trust him. Isn't it true that we often try to blame our roles or our circumstances for problems that really begin with our refusal or inability to believe God and trust him? That's a common problem, I think—the fear of really trusting God with everything in our lives. My particular fear was that God would demand I give up my goals of a successful career and a marriage with "Mr. Right" and substitute some dreadful life of loneliness and drudgery.

So I took over the management of my life, with all the various roles that were expected of me. And in short order, I had my identity pretty well confused. I switched hats as my roles demanded. Sometimes I wore the "Mother Hat," sometimes the "Business Hat"; then I would switch to the "Female Hat" and the "Christian Hat" when appropriate. But the roles did not blend, and my priorities were often poor.

Lifestyle Rationalization

I was frequently a different person under the different hats. That role juggling fostered hypocrisy in many areas and led to lifestyle rationalizations on my part. You know what lifestyle rationalization is, don't you? It is when you convince yourself that what you are doing is necessary for success or happiness—whatever drive or desire is uppermost at the time—and therefore your actions are justifiable. It's all very similar to situation ethics. I rationalized that certain social practices were necessary in the high-powered sales business I was in, and though incompatible with my "Christian Hat," they were necessary when wearing my "Business Hat." When I wore my "Female Hat," my search-for-a-man hat, I rationalized behavior that was totally unacceptable with my "Mother Hat" or my "Christian Hat."

Lifestyle rationalization is not unusual when we're juggling roles and confused as to our real identity. You can spot a great deal of it these days among Christians. My own identity crisis had led me to an unacceptable and sinful lifestyle rationalization.

A Turning Point

There came a turning point in my life where I saw the futility of this role-juggling, and I found the hat switching was more than I could handle. The best description of the turmoil inside me then is that I was like an emotional yo-yo! The ups and downs became more and more extreme, and the downs began to last longer than the ups. My guilt and failure to achieve my self-centered goals for each of my roles gradually took their toll. This ten-year struggle caused me to come unglued.

My brightest hopes of being superwoman were crushed. My job suffered, my role as a mother suffered, my relationships suffered, my self-image suffered. I was no longer performing well in any of my roles; I was confused, and I was desperate. It was this desperation that finally brought me to that crucial turning point.

What actually changed was my mind-set. I was so desperate for peace and contentment that they became my goals and objectives. And where could I turn for peace? Obviously, running my own life was not the answer. I had tried that for ten years and failed miserably. So, at the end of my rope, I said to God, "I'm willing to do anything and be anything, if you will only give me peace."

For the first time in many years I truly wanted to be in a right relationship with God more than anything else. This was, finally, the identity that took priority over everything else for me. I was wrong to struggle for such a long time and to wait until I was almost without hope before turning to God for the answer. How I appreciate his long-suffering and patience with me! I continue to marvel at how he could have put up with me that long time. But the story of the prodigal son's return tells us that we have just such a heavenly Father, who gladly receives us back even when we've wasted years and resources and opportunities.

Now that I see the miraculous changes he has brought to my life, I ask myself why I did not trust him sooner. The answer that comes back is that I did not really understand who God is and therefore how trustworthy he is. I had been taught the basics of Christianity from my earliest days, had graduated from a Christian college, and was active in church all my life. The fault does not lie with my teaching but rather with my dullness of understanding and the satanic fear of trusting God that was controlling my life. This long identity struggle was the result of my refusal to trust God with my life's direction.

Life-Changing Principles

I believe the principles and truths that changed my life at that turning point and gave me the key to finding my true identity are basic and helpful for anyone who is still struggling with an identity problem. They work for all who are changing hats, shifting identities, trying to be what they think they should be or what they think they want to be, and never finding their true identity.

These principles aren't found in new philosophies, new psychological theories, or new therapeutic treatments. Surprised? We think we've come up with a new disorder, peculiar to our high-tech, high-stress, high-powered generation—and we call it an identity crisis. But our new disorder is just an old problem called carnality or self-centeredness or walking after the flesh and not after the Spirit. We try to put a new name on it, thereby giving it some respectability, and find new cures for it. But anything short of God's principles and God's solution is a very short-term, unsatisfying answer.

The three basic principles that began to go from my head to my heart are simple beyond belief. Undoubtedly, most of you will nod your head in agreement as you read them. They are not new. Many, many people far more eloquent than I have stated them much better. Saints through the ages have proclaimed their truth. I believe with all my heart that if you will truly believe these three simple truths and implement them in your everyday life, you will put an end to your identity struggle, your life will change, and those fears of trusting God will be no more.

Understand Who God Is

First, I had to really begin to understand who this God is that I claimed to serve and worship. Isaiah 44:6, 8 tells us our God is the only God:

> Thus says the LORD, the King of Israel
> And his Redeemer, the LORD of hosts:
> "I am the first and I am the last,
> And there is no God besides Me. . . .
> Is there any God besides Me,
> Or is there any other Rock?
> I know of none."

In verse 24 we see that he is God the Creator.

> Thus says the LORD, your Redeemer, and the one who formed
>   you from the womb,
> "I, the LORD, am the maker of all things,
> Stretching out the heavens by Myself,
> And spreading out the earth all alone."

Our God is all powerful and does what he pleases:

> I know that the LORD is great,
> And that our Lord is above all gods.
> Whatever the LORD pleases, He does,
> In heaven and in earth, in the seas and in all deeps.
>   Psalm 135:5–6

He is holy and he is perfect. He does not make mistakes: "One called out to another and said, 'Holy, Holy, Holy, is the LORD of hosts, the whole earth is full of His glory'" (Isa. 6:3). Matthew 5:48 echoes this same truth, "Therefore you are to be perfect, as your heavenly Father is perfect."

Either this God we claim to serve is as these verses describe him, or he is not. Do you believe he is the only God, the creator, all powerful, and perfect? I recognize how basic this is, but that is step one in coming to a place where you can really trust him without fear.

Understand How God Feels about Us

If we are convinced that God's character, power, and personality are as described, the next important issue is to understand how this same God feels about us. After all, we are but specks in a great mass of humanity and in a vast universe. Do we make any difference to God? Again, Scripture gives us an answer:

Why do you say, O Jacob, and assert, O Israel,
"My way is hidden from the LORD,
And the justice due me escapes the notice of my God?"
Do you not know? Have you not heard?
The Everlasting God, the LORD, the Creator of the ends of the
    earth
Does not become weary or tired.
His understanding is inscrutable.

Isaiah 40:27–28

These verses tell us that, in spite of the vast number of people who live or ever have lived or will live, God does not lose track of you and me!

Matthew 10:30 tells us, "The very hairs of your head are all numbered." Every time we brush our hair we can be reminded that God has just recomputed all those lost hairs—and furthermore, he knows which numbers were lost, and he is keeping a running total at all times! Who else would care how many hairs are on our heads? This gives us some idea of how much God cares for us.

In Matthew 10:29 and 31 we read that even the sparrows—those plentiful, common birds we see all the time—are under the care of God. He knows each one that falls to the ground. Can we not believe that if God cares so much about sparrows, he cares much more about us? Psalm 139:1–4 reiterates God's intimate care for each of us:

O LORD, Thou hast searched me and known me.
Thou dost know when I sit down and when I rise up;

Thou dost understand my thought from afar.
Thou dost scrutinize my path and my lying down,
And art intimately acquainted with all my ways.

Would even our mothers care to know how many times we sit down or stand up today? Yet God cares, and he knows and understands even our far-off thoughts—the ones we do not understand ourselves. He is intimately acquainted and concerned with everything we do, every place we go. If we believe the Scriptures we've quoted, we must believe this.

The God we worship, the one and only God, the eternal God, the God of all power, wisdom, and holiness—this very God really cares about you and me with a care and concern unsurpassed by any other person in the world.

Understand God's Plan for Us

God's plans for us are always superior to any other plans. If you believe those first two principles, you cannot logically deny this one. Therefore, you can trust him. Not only can you trust him, it is the only logical thing to do. Nothing else makes any sense. Just look at what the Scriptures tell us about God's intentions toward us:

> No good thing does He withhold from those who walk uprightly.
>
> Psalm 84:11

> Now to Him who is able to do exceeding abundantly beyond all that we ask or think, according to the power that works within us.
>
> Ephesians 3:20

> For to those who fear Him, there is no want. . . . But they who seek the LORD shall not be in want of any good thing.
>
> Psalm 34:9–10

The irrefutable, logical conclusion is clear. There simply can be no middle ground. If we believe with our hearts, not just our heads, that God is God, eternal, all powerful, holy, and perfect; that this very God cares for us more than any earthly being could ever care, and that his plans for our lives are far better than anything we could engineer on our own, there can be no fear on our part to trust him. He can be nothing but trustworthy. He will lead us into the best paths. To fail to relinquish the control of our lives to him would be foolhardy and disastrous.

If this is so simple and so logical, why are so many Christians still refusing to really trust God, as I did for many years? I think it's because we become victims of conflicting messages from our three enemies: the world, the flesh, and the devil.

The world tells us: "Do your own thing," "Find yourself," "Do what feels good," "Go for it!" The flesh says to us: "You deserve happiness, and you have a right to run your life the way you want it." The devil says: "If you trust God, you most surely will be led into some terrible life."

I listened to these voices, and I forsook consistent study of God's Word and prayer, and fear took over. I became convinced that totally trusting God was too risky. It was meant only for those few people who somehow have the courage to go into full-time Christian service. Without realizing what I was doing, my actions said that I believed I could trust myself better than I could trust God. I am beginning to realize what arrogance it is on my part to refuse to trust God. If I really believe the three basic principles outlined above, to fail to trust him at every turn in my life is a grave and serious sin. It is pride at its very worst.

Comprehending how totally trustworthy God is leads us to yield to his total lordship in our lives. And this takes the monkey off our back! It gives us a marvelous freedom, because we are no longer responsible for managing our own destinies. Someone far more qualified is now in charge—the God of all the ages—and we can be absolutely sure that his plan will be the best thing for us.

I made up my mind that Jesus Christ was worthy of my total commitment, and regardless of the cost, he would take first place. My identity began to change: No longer did I think of myself as a woman with several roles to blend and balance, switching identities like hats, but I saw myself as a woman with one obligation—to be what God wanted me to be. The identity crisis began to come to an end.

Oh, I still had to go to work every day, and I was still a woman and a mother. The roles had not gone away. But they fell into order as I began to put into practice what I had known for a long time—that I was bought with a price, I belonged to Jesus, I was not my own, and my identity was simply to be an obedient servant of my Lord. This certainly did not all happen overnight. It was, and is, a continuing process. But it began with that moment when I gave my will over to him and decided that I could truly trust him with my future and with my identity.

This has made sweeping changes in all my roles. As I began, little by little, to apply what I was learning to my everyday job, that job took on a new significance. It was a part of God's plan for me and no longer a separate, sectionalized part of my life. So I could trust God with all the details of my job and my career.

I wanted to be a better mother than ever before, and my daughter, who is now grown and married, has confirmed to me that the improvement in my mothering responsibilities has been significant. She now has a role model more important than that of a successful career woman; she now sees a mother who is learning how to let Jesus control every part of her life. And I'm thankful to report that she now works on the staff of The Christian Working Woman as manager of operations. How special of the Lord to give me this confirming touch that he can bring beauty out of our ashes.

Instead of trying to find myself as a woman, my desire is to be a "woman after God's own heart." I began to learn that Jesus was very capable of drawing together all the parts of my identity and making me into a whole, fulfilled woman.

An End to the Struggle

Are you struggling with your identity? Do you see yourself as a person with several roles, trying to play a balancing act in prioritizing them and plagued with guilt and frustration because you know you are not succeeding too well? Is your identity out of focus, and are you wearing hats that aren't very comfortable—maybe some you know you should not be wearing at all? Well, I want to encourage you, because there is an answer. It is the same answer it has been for ages past, and it is equally effective for the special needs of working women as it is for everyone else.

Here it is, very simply. All of those multiple roles you're struggling with have to be replaced by one single identity—that of a woman who desires to be only and exactly what God has planned for her to be. That means giving up your will and trusting the God of the universe with your life and your future. When you do this, the other roles will take their proper place. Jesus knows how important it is to you to be successful in your job and in all the other areas of your life. He does not condemn you for that. It's just that he knows that unless he is the center of your life, you are headed for disappointment, confusion, and failure. Your identity crisis ends when you identify Jesus Christ as the central focus of your life and determine that all other roles must come under his management and his direction.

That's the basic principle that began to change my life, and I am confident it will work for you too. And when that commitment to Jesus Christ is in place, we'll find answers for the many confusing struggles we encounter as working women. It is my earnest prayer that if you are experiencing this fear of trusting God, and if you are confused about your identity, you will just now relinquish your will to our loving, all-powerful God, who longs to be gracious to you and waits to have compassion on you.

2

Self-Esteem:
Making the Most
of Your Talents

An examination of self-identity quite naturally leads to thoughts of self-esteem. Women have credits to their names now that were undreamed of a generation ago. We have successes to talk about that our mothers could never have imagined. By all the world's standards, we've made considerable progress on all fronts, having been liberated from our limited, confining roles and allowed to pursue most any role that suits our fancy. How then do we regard ourselves?

We've been told that low self-esteem is a prevalent problem among American women today. Do you, like me, find that difficult to understand? In the early 1960s, when Betty Friedan wrote *The Feminine Mystique,* she proclaimed that our low self-esteem was due to our limited roles and opportunities. Her basic message was that if women were allowed to be more than just wives and mothers and could achieve identities of their own instead of simply assuming the identities of their husbands or even their children, then they would no longer feel the frustration of low self-esteem. You and I have watched the opportunities open up. But frustration is still with us. In fact, the level of self-esteem has gone down rather than up in the last two decades.

What Is Self-Esteem?

First, let's define what we mean by self-esteem. We have opinions of other people, and when those opinions are positive and good, we say that we hold those people in high esteem. Conversely, we can have negative opinions of people that cause us to hold them in low esteem. Consciously or unconsciously, we also have an opinion of ourselves. And that opinion is our self-esteem. Opinions, as we all know, are not necessarily based on facts. The dictionary says that an opinion is a "belief stronger than impression and less strong than positive knowledge." So the opinion we have of ourselves—our self-esteem—can be accurate or inaccurate.

Your Own Self-Esteem

What is your opinion of yourself? If there were such a thing as a scale of self-esteem, where would you fit in? Would you be on the low end, with your head hung low, feeling totally worthless and a complete failure? Or would you find yourself at the other end, with head held high, proud of your accomplishments, confident that you can do anything you want to do, unafraid to tackle anything, assertive, successful, and proud of it? Quite likely you fall at some point in between those two descriptions. Are you in negative territory or positive territory? I'm asking you to rate what your opinion is of yourself, whether accurate or not. Many times we hold onto inaccurate opinions, even while recognizing some of their inaccuracies.

Our opinions on any given subject have been shaped by various factors. They may have been formed over a long period of time or quickly. They may be based on good input—accurate information, or bad input—inaccurate information. They may be right or wrong conclusions. But something has influenced those opinions.

Self-esteem can be based on comparisons. Frequently, we compare ourselves with what we think we should be, what others have told us we should be, what society thinks we should be. A great portion of our self-esteem is based on comparison with some other person or standard.

Now think: To what or whom do you compare yourself? Do you look at all the so-called beautiful women today, as displayed by television and Hollywood, and conclude that all beautiful women are thin? Then if you are not thin, are you not beautiful? Is that a standard of comparison you use? Do you compare yourself with what your parents said you should be? Do you compare yourself with a friend, someone at work, society's current image of the successful working woman?

Self-esteem can be based on what others have told us about ourselves. Part of our opinion of ourselves is based on what others have told us. This could be nonverbal as well as verbal, since their actions may have told us what their words did not. For example, did your parents give you lots of praise and cause you to have good feelings about yourself, or did they constantly belittle and criticize you? Or something in between? Have you had a boss who has really raised your self-esteem by telling you what a good worker you are? Or to the contrary? Do you have a husband who thinks you "hung the moon," as we say in the South, or one who is never happy with what you do?

I think of a person I know whose mother was extremely capable. Whatever her mother attempted, she excelled in it. My friend's mother criticized everything she tried to do, and throughout her childhood she was continually reminded that what she did could have been done better by her mother. Not surprisingly, my friend grew up with serious doubts about her ability to do things well. Her self-esteem was greatly affected by this verbal and nonverbal input from her mother.

Conversely, my father has always told me he thought I was capable of being anything I wanted to be. As a result, I've always been eager to try new things. His verbal positive input has made a difference in my self-esteem.

All of this input from other people goes into formulating your opinions about yourself.

Self-esteem can be based on our experiences. Did you win the title of "Most Likely to Succeed" when you graduated from high school? That experience could contribute favorably to your self-esteem. Did you make good grades in college? That influences your self-esteem. Did you get fired from a job? Such an experience and other failures and successes are all part of the process that creates your opinion of yourself.

I hope that you have a clear understanding of what self-esteem is and, if you've never thought about it before, that you're beginning to get a picture of what has formed your present state of self-esteem—whether it is low, high, or something in between.

Why the Low Self-Esteem Epidemic?

We mentioned earlier that low self-esteem is called the most prevalent problem of women today. Why would that be true, in a period when we should feel better about ourselves because of all our new accomplishments and opportunities? In thinking about it, I have come to believe that the following factors play a large part in this problem.

• *The Superwoman complex.* Much more is expected of women today. The Superwoman complex has hit hard. Whereas in the past, society was perfectly accepting of us if we were housewives and mothers, or perhaps in some acceptable female occupation such as teacher, nurse, secretary, librarian, and so forth, now those accomplishments are not considered nearly as commendable. What was a short time ago a perfectly acceptable standard for performance for a woman has now become almost an indictment. "You only want to be a mother and wife?" "You aren't interested in being a vice president?" The standards to which we compare ourselves are more stringent and demanding.

Furthermore, we're expected to do what we did before in

addition to taking on these many new roles open to us. This Superwoman phenomenon has gotten to many of us and negatively affected our self-esteem.

•*Divorce.* With the divorce rate increasing as it has over the past two decades, many women's self-esteem has suffered considerably. Divorce is tough! You feel as though you're wearing a sign around your neck that says, "I'm a failure: a failure at the thing I should excel in—being a wife." And for the women who experienced rejection with their divorce, when their husbands left them for someone else, this is doubly damaging to their self-esteem.

•*Abused and battered women.* I've read that we can expect from 25 to 50 percent of women to experience some kind of abuse in their lives. It is estimated that one out of four children suffers abuse today. Certainly, abuse and violence in general have increased in our society, and women are easy targets. Perhaps our new assertiveness has threatened men more than before and that has been part of the cause for the increase in abuse—whether sexual, physical, or emotional.

Without question, abuse has devastating effects on women. I'm just beginning to realize the terrible pain and suffering many women, women I personally know, have struggled with because of abuse.

•*Singleness.* And then, more of us than ever before are single. We either marry later or not at all, taking care of ourselves and not sharing our identity with a man. And yet our society still looks at an unmarried woman as slightly inferior, not quite making it. There is a stigma for the single woman, especially in Christian circles. Frankly, I think single women are as much the cause as the victim of that stigma, because we keep thinking of ourselves as incomplete unless married. And we keep behaving in ways that say to the world, "I'm desperate; I need a husband." Many single women live with this gnawing feeling inside that until they get married, they fall short of acceptable standards of success as women. And that can have very negative effects on our self-esteem.

•*Sexual permissiveness.* Another important reason for our declining self-esteem is the new sexual freedom that has become prevalent in the last few decades. No longer is it necessary for any commitment to exist in a sexual relationship. Not only is marriage not necessary, no type of commitment is required. God's principle of limiting sexual relationships to those who are married is now considered absolutely unreasonable and outdated by our society.

This sexual permissiveness goes totally against the nature of women, in my opinion. Whether we admit it or not, our inborn reaction and inclination is that when we give ourselves to a man in a physical relationship we give our hearts and our emotions, and we expect and need commitment from that man in return.

Women today, in trying to be "with it," try to ignore these natural reactions and needs, and give themselves indiscriminately, without any commitment. I believe this tears at a woman's self-esteem with devastating effects. The lack of any commitment or long-term relationship in these physical involvements, while quite acceptable in today's environment, is not acceptable to a woman's self-esteem. It causes a woman to lose self-respect and lower her opinion of herself.

•*The "Me Generation."* Of great significance, to my mind, is the fact that for the past few decades our society has been inundated with the humanistic point of view. And that humanism has caused us to focus our attention almost exclusively on ourselves. There's no question about it, we are the "Me Generation." We want to do what's right for us, we want to do our own thing, we want to grab all the gusto since we go around only once in this world. We have become extremely self-absorbed.

That self-absorption is very appealing to our human nature, and we've all been caught up in it. We think of ourselves more than ever before and we place an extremely high importance on our well-being. As we've begun focusing more on ourselves, we've become increasingly vulnerable to our own failures, inadequacies, the bad breaks we've had in life, or the unfair treatment we've received. All of these negative things take on greater significance as we concentrate on ourselves. And the result? An increased negative effect on our self-esteem.

We can see how all these forces combine to create an atmosphere conducive to a lowering of women's self-esteem. But the question remains, what can we do to reverse the trend?

Solving the Problem of Low Self-Esteem

The word *self-esteem* does not appear in the Bible. Does that mean the Bible has nothing to say about it? Well, since God put us all together, I believe he understands us better than anyone. Therefore, his Book should be the very best source there is on anything having to do with us as individuals. I believe the Bible has some very good answers for us. I'd like to look again at the causes of low self-esteem that I've listed and see what the Word of God has to tell us about each of them.

The Superwoman Complex

What is the root cause of the Superwoman complex? I believe it results from comparing ourselves to what we think we should be or what society tells us we should be—which is to be able to do anything and everything and to do it very well. So in order to be acceptable, we looked around and decided to be superwomen.

Have you done that? Have you come up on the short end? Are you aware that as a Christian woman, you are free from having to compare yourself with other people? Remember what Jesus taught us. After the resurrection, when Jesus prophesied to Peter that he would be called on to suffer for him, Peter turned and looked at John and said, "What about this man?" Jesus said to Peter, "What is that to you? You follow me" (see John 21:21–22). Jesus is clearly telling Peter not to compare himself with others. The same is true for us today. Jesus would say to us, "What difference does that make to you? Your job is to follow me, without comparing your circumstances, your abilities, your position, your background, your education, your age, your looks, or anything else with anyone else. Your duty is simply to follow me."

He gave us another clear message in the parable of the talents (see Matt. 25:14–28). I'm going to examine this parable in some detail, because it is relevant to other areas of discussion in this book.

As he was leaving on a journey, a master left his three servants with different talents. To one he gave five talents, to one two, and to the other one he gave one talent. The servant with the five talents went right to work and doubled his talents to ten. Likewise, the servant with two talents doubled his talents to four. But the servant with one talent reacted quite differently. He went away and dug a hole in the ground and buried his one talent.

It's quite likely that this man with one talent was miffed because he had only one talent and the others had more. I think he made a comparison and felt cheated because he didn't start out with as much as the others. And that comparison could have caused him to lose confidence in himself. Don't you imagine that he might well have felt very inadequate about having only one talent and doubted his ability to be able to do anything with it?

Well, what happens when the master returns? He calls these servants to account for what they've done with their talents. The first two report that they have doubled their money, and the master gives to each of them the same reply: "Well done, good and faithful slave; you were faithful with a few things, I will put you in charge of many things; enter into the joy of your master" (vv. 21, 23).

Even though one slave had more than twice what the other slave had, they got the same reward and the same commendation. The master didn't say, "Well, the ten-talent slave is obviously better than the four-talent slave, because he has more talents. Therefore, he gets first place and the four-talent guy gets second place." He did not compare their results or demand that the two-talent servant do as much as the five-talent servant did. Because both of them had diligently done well with what they started with, they were regarded as being equally successful.

But notice our one-talent servant—the one who went out and buried his money. When the master asked him for a report, he said, "Master, I knew you to be a hard man, reaping where you did not sow, and gathering where you scattered no seed. And I was afraid, and went away and hid your talent in the ground; see, you have what is yours" (vv. 24–25).

Does his answer make sense to you? This poor servant was not thinking very straight. He knows his master is interested in increasing his money, but instead of doing what he knows will please the master, he hides the money. He's so afraid of losing that one talent, he buries it.

Now, if you didn't know the rest of this parable, and you were to write the ending, what would you write? I think most of us would write something like this: "Oh, well, that's okay. I know how you feel. And besides, you just had one talent anyway; it's no big deal. But listen, next time why don't you look at what these other fellows did and try to be more like them. You need to try a little harder next time."

Let me quote the ending that Jesus gave to this story:

> You wicked, lazy slave, you knew that I reap where I did not sow, and gather where I scattered no seed. Then you ought to have put my money in the bank, and on my arrival I would have received my money back with interest. Therefore take away the talent from him, and give it to the one who has the ten talents.
>
> verses 26–28

What? He called this fellow wicked and lazy! Can you imagine? No sympathy whatsoever for the fact that he had only one talent to begin with. And why is he upset over one silly talent? After all, the other two servants earned an additional seven talents for him.

What is the principle Jesus is teaching us here? Look at it very carefully because it is most important: *Jesus does not compare us with other people.* His standard of acceptable performance is that we take what we have been given and we do a lot with it. His rewards and commendations are not based on how much we accomplish, how far up the ladder we climb, but rather they are based on comparing where we started with where we finish.

When we compare ourselves with other people, other criteria, other standards, we will become demoralized and frustrated. Like the man with one talent, we'll give up before we get started. We'll just tuck our tails between our legs and go home and sit and wait.

You and I are responsible to our Master to multiply the talents we've been given, but he will not compare our results with those of other people. What he expects of me is not what he expects of you in actual results. But he does expect all of us to multiply our talents, whatever they are.

Jesus gave us this powerful illustration so that we will understand his priorities and standards of performance. He will have no sympathy for the less-talented, less-educated person who uses that as an excuse to bury herself and do nothing. He will have no sympathy for the person who uses her bad background or bad breaks as an excuse for sitting home and feeling sorry for herself. But he does not expect a one-talent person to do what the five-talent person does.

By the same token, we can compare ourselves with others and decide we're pretty hot stuff. You know, we can always find someone lower on the totem pole than we are. And if we make comparisons of that sort, we can make the mistake of thinking more highly of ourselves than we should. Then, taking our leisure like the rabbit in the famous race with the turtle, we also will fail to use our talents properly. Jesus also taught us that to whom much is given, much is required (Luke 12:48).

As long as we keep comparing ourselves to other people and their standards, our self-esteem will never be healthy. It will either be too low or too high. But by taking the abilities and opportunities given to us and multiplying whatever they are, we'll find that our opinion of ourselves will become more accurate and realistic—and healthier.

Divorce

For those of you, like me, who have gone through divorce, I have good news for you: It is not the unpardonable sin. Whatever the cause of your divorce, whether it was your idea or not, as long as you've confessed any sin that may have been on your part, you are not condemned by the Lord. In fact, he says he doesn't even remember our sins once they are confessed. And hold on to this wonderful verse, Isaiah 61:3 (KJV):

> To appoint unto them that mourn in Zion, to give unto them beauty for ashes, the oil of joy for mourning, the garment of praise for the spirit of heaviness; that they might be called trees of right-eousness, the planting of the Lord, that he might be glorified.

Your ashes can be turned into beauty, your mourning into joy. That heavy spirit you carry around with you can become a spirit of praise. And you—yes you, a divorced woman—can be called a tree of righteousness, you can become the Lord's plant, and he will be glorified through you.

Ask God to help you shed the heavy garment of failure that we divorced people tend to wear. God is no respecter of persons. He doesn't favor a non-divorced person over a divorced person. Your life is not ruined. You can become what God wants you to be. Oh, do believe this.

And if you experienced rejection as a result of that divorce, remember this: Jesus Christ has promised never to leave you or forsake you. NEVER. Now, consider how special you are, that Jesus Christ will never leave you. I know how rejection hurts, but Jesus can heal it. Wrap yourself in his love, and constantly think of the fact that he will always be with you. Nothing will ever separate you from Christ, if you know him as your Savior. Concentrating on Christ's love for you can heal those wounds caused by divorce and rejection and can restore your self-esteem.

Abused and Battered Women

If you are a part of those statistics on abused and battered women, my heart reaches out to you with great compassion. I can only imagine how deep the wounds must be and how difficult it is to find healing and relief. I know that most abused women are made to believe that they suffered that abuse because they were worthless, even bad people. One of the biggest hurdles for abused women is the gnawing feeling that they deserve what happened to them, that there was some evil in them that caused the abuse.

The healing you need is not a quick fix, I know that. That's why we have to establish support groups on a long-term basis. You may well need some professional help from a Christian counselor to be able to deal with past pain as well as present difficulties.

I would just say to you, as one Christian woman to another, that I know you can find healing in Jesus. I know that he understands your suffering, that God is outraged at what has happened to you. He will have his vengeance on those who abuse children and women, and it will be dreadful.

Meanwhile, you must cope with the damage that abuse has done to your opinion of yourself, your self-esteem. The best thing you can do is to saturate yourself with the Word of God. As I've talked to women who have experienced abuse, I realize that those who have really spent time in God's Word are far more capable of recovering from the damage done to them than those who have not.

This will do several things for you. It will show you how much God loves you and how important you are to him. And it will give you a basis for reprogramming your mind. Your memories and your thinking need a new way of looking at life, and God's Word is the best input for that. Remember, God sees you as a lovely creature, made by him in a special way. The abuse you may have suffered has not caused him to find you unlovely or unlovable. He affirms you as a woman whom he loves, and he cares intimately about you. I know that, as you can begin to find your completeness in him, he will have healing for those terrible hurts. And he can heal the damage done to your self-esteem. There's nothing too hard for our God. He longs to be gracious to you.

One friend of mine who had suffered abuse in her childhood shared with me how God was healing her. For years she had carried the hurt and pain from the abuse, and it had severely damaged her view of herself. It was also taking a major toll on her marriage and her family relationships.

Finally, she came back to the Lord and turned the pain over to him. She determined in her heart to focus on knowing the Lord. She said to me, "Mary, I can either magnify my past and the pain of abuse or I can magnify the Lord in my life. I've decided to magnify the Lord." She got back into a regular pattern of Bible study, and she began to reach out to others with help and comfort.

Because of her past, she is able to comfort and help many women with similar experiences, and God is using her painful past for good. She is still confronting that past, has had some conversations with her parents, and hopes to be able to get more of it out in the open. But her focus is no longer on her past; it is on getting to know God and magnifying him in her life. And that has brought her more healing and help than anything else could have done.

Often, people with painful pasts expect some earthly counselor to give them answers, or they aren't willing to give up the resentment; they aren't willing to forgive. Only Jesus can heal you and take away the resentment and give you the power to forgive. While he sometimes uses people to help us, his Word can be our refuge and strength and needs to be our first choice for counsel and healing.

Singleness

If, because you are single, you have the uneasy feeling that you're not quite a real person yet, your self-esteem has undoubtedly suffered as a result. I truly understand this, because I spent the first ten years after my divorce struggling with this feeling of inadequacy because I wasn't married. I felt that if I could marry the kind of man I sought, everybody would sit up and take notice and say, "Wow, Mary Whelchel must be really something. Look at the man who married her." I wanted a man to wear as my badge of acceptability. My self-esteem was suffering, and I was certain that the right man was the cure for that problem.

Let me tell you briefly what I have learned. There is not a man on earth who can give you the total affirmation that you are looking for. You can ask the most happily married woman you know, and she will tell you, if she is honest, that many times her husband does not and cannot meet her needs.

The only man who can give you complete affirmation is Christ Jesus. If you really want a badge to wear, wear his badge. How much better can you get? To say you belong to him has to be one of the best credentials you can ever have.

I see so many single women doing what I did for so long, and my heart breaks for you. I know you're looking for acceptance, but I so want you to believe me when I tell you that you don't have to be married to be fulfilled as a woman. Listen to what the apostle Paul tells us in 1 Corinthians 7:34: "And the woman who is unmarried, and the virgin, is concerned about the things of the Lord, that she may be holy both in body and spirit; but one who is married is concerned about the things of the world, how she may please her husband."

To get the full context of this verse, you need to read that whole chapter. Paul doesn't condemn marriage, but he does tell us that we have more freedom when we are not married. Would any married woman deny that? And Paul is telling us that to remain unmarried can indeed be very praiseworthy and honorable.

Why is it that we never look at this Scripture and concentrate on its truth? Ever heard a sermon on this passage? Yes, marriage is a wonderful thing. Yes, the family is the basic building block of our society. But that does not mean that the unmarried have less credibility or purpose. Just the opposite! We should be able to be more concerned about eternal matters because we are not married.

If you're a single Christian woman, burdened with the image of yourself as incomplete until married, please read 1 Corinthians 7:34 again and again and believe its truth. You can be so very special in God's kingdom. Hold your head high and declare yourself married to the Lord, and go forward. You're not just okay; you're special!

Sexual Permissiveness

It's my opinion that many women have suffered a great deal of damage to their self-esteem because of their permissive attitude toward sexual relationships with men. I know that this is perfectly acceptable in our society today, but it is not acceptable by God's principles. Sex is reserved for marriage. And not because God is a gigantic killjoy who wants to make our life difficult, but because he knows that this intimate relationship apart from commitment can do nothing but harm us. And you can see that very harm happening to women all around you, maybe even to you.

When a woman gives herself physically without the commitment of marriage, she not only is committing a sin, she is dealing death blows to her self-esteem. It may seem different at first. The attention may cause you to think that you're really special for awhile. But before it's over, you'll suffer greatly from these illegitimate relationships. God's principles are for our good, not to make life difficult. There is only one answer to this problem: Determine to live a life of purity, regardless of the price you must pay. It will bring healing to your damaged self-esteem.

The "Me Generation"

I think all of us have to plead guilty to the problem of being self-absorbed. First, we're born that way. Ever notice that you don't have to teach children to be selfish? They come by it naturally. And second, our particular generation has had a double whammy of self-absorption because of the current trend toward humanistic thinking.

Biblical principles are in exact opposition to this intense concentration on who we are, what makes us tick, and taking care of number one.

> Jesus said to his disciples, "If anyone would come after me, he must deny himself and take up his cross and follow me."
> Matthew 16:24 NIV

> For through the grace given to me I say to every man among you not to think more highly of himself than he ought to think; but to think so as to have sound judgment, as God has allotted to each a measure of faith.
> Romans 12:3

Do nothing out of selfish ambition or vain conceit, but in humility consider others better than yourselves.

Philippians 2:3 NIV

Rather than telling us to focus on ourselves, Jesus tells us to deny ourselves. Rather than dressing up this old self of ours and showing everyone how wonderful we are, Jesus tells us to die to ourselves. There is nothing in the teaching of our Master that would cause us to pursue a course of promoting our own selves whatsoever. He taught us to be servants, as he was a servant.

While there are understandable reasons that women struggle with low self-esteem, the cure for the problem is not to become more and more self-focused. A healthy self-esteem allows us to forget about ourselves and invest our lives in other people. We need to have an accurate understanding of who we are as Christian women and base our opinions of ourselves on that understanding. God has created us in his image. Think about that. Because we belong to him, as we read in Ephesians, we are seated in the heavenlies with Christ Jesus, we are heirs of God and joint heirs with Jesus Christ. Think of what that means.

When I think about who I am in Jesus and because of Jesus, the rest of my background and failures start to diminish in importance. So what if I don't fit the world's mold of what beautiful should be. So what if I don't measure up to someone else's standards of acceptability. So what if I'm not a superwoman. So what if my accomplishments are less than other women. No one can condemn me, because Jesus doesn't condemn me. Read what Paul wrote to the Romans:

Who would dare to accuse us, whom God has chosen? God himself has declared us free from sin. Who is in a position to condemn? Only Christ Jesus, and Christ died for us, Christ also rose for us, Christ reigns in power for us, Christ prays for us!

Romans 8:33–34 PHILLIPS

If someone is condemning you—or you are condemning yourself—and your self-esteem is at rock bottom because you don't think you measure up, will you memorize this Scripture and believe it? Nobody has a right to accuse you of anything, not even yourself. Nobody can accuse you except Christ. But the wonderful news is that Christ doesn't accuse you. He died for you, he rose for you, he reigns for you, he prays for you! The first verse of that same eighth chapter of Romans says that "no condemnation now hangs over the head of those who are 'in' Christ Jesus" (PHILLIPS). Who is "in" Christ Jesus? Those who have accepted him as their Savior. Are you in Christ Jesus? If the answer is yes, then you are not condemned by him.

Now, based on this incredible truth, we need to accept who we are in Christ and then move on to other things. We've got to conquer this absorption with self if we're ever going to be able to reach this world with Christ's love. When you start to feel confident that you are special because you belong to the Lord Jesus, then you can start to forget yourself and reach out to others. This means that we must learn to deny ourselves, to die to our own desires, to think of others as more important than we are, to become servants, to love our neighbors as ourselves.

Quite frankly, I believe we have lost perspective on this whole issue of self-esteem. We tend to give it too much importance. Our educational system is riddled with the need to improve students' self-esteem instead of educating them! It has become a catchall excuse for any problem that anyone has, and we've lost the biblical view of self.

One of the great paradoxes of Scripture is that when we die to ourselves, we become alive to God. Self is not the solution; self is the problem! And the smartest thing we can do, as well as the most biblical thing, is to stop focusing on self-esteem and start focusing on getting to know God and pleasing him.

When we start to reach out to others and care about other people, regardless of how needy we may be, we're going to discover that the healing process starts. That low self-esteem problem we've been battling will never be won by getting more promotions or a face-lift or losing weight or going back to school. Not that there is anything wrong with any of those things, and certainly they can help us feel better about ourselves. But they are only Band-Aids. They're not the cure.

Many of us have become prisoners to this issue of self-esteem, trying to find our completeness in ourselves instead of finding ourselves in Christ. We're like the man with the one talent, who sat in his corner and buried his talent, full of anger, full of envy, feeling very inadequate and too frightened to try to do anything for fear he would lose what he had. We're useless to the purposes of God's kingdom when we're so absorbed by self.

I want to stand before God and hear, "Well done, good and faithful servant," don't you? We can, you know. Every one of us has that potential. But we must set our will and our mind to accept ourselves where we are, and then go on from there.

3

Ambition, Success, and Money

My friend, Jane, who is a nurse, made an unusual job change. After years of pursuing her career and working diligently and successfully to be a first-rate nurse, she decided to leave nursing and become a secretary in the hospital. That move on her part meant a significant cut in salary, and in most people's view, it was a step down the career ladder. Why did she do it? Didn't she like nursing? Had she had a bad experience that soured her on her career? No, she enjoyed nursing and may go back to it someday. But because of the schedule required of her as a nurse, she could never take any responsibility at church and had to miss many church functions and opportunities for service. After much thought and prayer, she felt God would have her choose a different career, at least for the present, in order to free up her schedule for serving in various ministries.

Many of her friends and associates, not understanding her motives, questioned the wisdom of this move on her part.

You see, the world expects all of us to be driven to pursue higher positions, greater success, and more money. To have a different set of ambitions and a different measurement of success is indeed unusual in our working environment.

Christians and non-Christians alike, male and female, can easily become absorbed in their ambition for business success. The desire for the money and power that are available at higher levels consumes many people, and their lives revolve around their professional ambitions. There is definitely an unspoken law in the business world that the norm for working people is to aspire to higher levels, to seek unending promotions, and to work continually to increase their earnings. Any amount of energy and time expended to these ends is intelligent, justified, and sensible.

I have observed this mind-set having two opposite and damaging effects on Christian women in the workplace. Many have bought into this ambition syndrome and have lost a proper perspective of what a Christian's priorities should be. Others, who have not been motivated to greater career ambitions, experience guilt and feelings of inadequacy because they aren't achievers. Let's examine both sides and try to determine how God's principles apply to this issue.

For a Christian in the working world, possessing or not possessing career ambitions is neither spiritual nor unspiritual. There is no scriptural directive that points us exclusively in either direction. Each category, however, has dangers about which you should be aware.

Ambition

In this relatively new era of equal opportunity, women are allowed to move ahead into jobs and positions that were closed to us only a few years ago. Indeed, we are expected to be ambitious, to strive for promotions, to forge new territory and set new records. Certainly, many of us have benefited from this new environment. I recognize that my lifestyle has been favorably affected by getting a job as a sales representative in a company where that job had been closed to women only a few short months before. That experience qualified me for other jobs, and the chain reaction enabled me to pursue a fairly successful career, with the monetary rewards and sense of self-importance that such accomplishments bring.

I for one am very thankful for being allowed to move ahead, since by personality I'm a competitive, energetic, achiever type. Being in the position, as a single mother, of having to work, it was in many ways a benefit to me to have the opportunity to advance. Had I been a generation older and faced similar circumstances, my options would have been greatly limited and that would have made a great difference in my standard of living.

So, for those of us who are inclined to push ahead in the working world, these new opportunities have been appreciated. It is not my purpose to lay a guilt trip on anyone who has taken advantage of these opportunities and advanced their careers as much as possible. Nothing in Scripture forbids or condemns career or monetary success. In fact, it is possible to be successful in a career or professional pursuit, to receive promotions, to attain high positions, and to excel in our jobs, and be absolutely in line with God's purposes for our lives. Joseph and Daniel are two outstanding examples of very successful businessmen, used greatly by God in their positions. Lydia is another person who used her success and her position to spread the gospel through her home into Europe. The Proverbs 31 woman had unusual business interests and success, and she is considered the role model of a godly woman.

Prioritizing Time and Energy

The Christian who is energetically pursuing career goals needs to be very much aware of the dangers and pitfalls that exist in that high-powered environment. Let's face it, highly ambitious, career-minded people are often workaholics. They devote inordinate amounts of time to their jobs and frequently have little time or energy left for anything else, including family, friends, church ministries, and so forth.

I could easily make a long list of people I know who have sacrificed many other important priorities in order to move their careers ahead. If they are Christians, they are not the people you call on at church to help with a project, because they never have time. If they somehow get pressured into accepting some church responsibility, they rarely fulfill their commitments because work has them tied up. They often neglect their friendships and family relationships, sometimes with terrible long-term damage to themselves and others.

Have you noticed how often the excuse "I had to work" is used as though there can be no contesting the fact that work must take first place? I've done it myself far too often, excusing myself from a commitment because "something came up at work." Undoubtedly, there are times when it is unavoidable. But the Christian who is never available or dependable for any type of service, whether church related or not, needs to seriously consider if this job pursuit is in line with God's purpose for her life.

We walk a fine line here, because in no way am I advocating lack of excellence. Excellence should be our trademark as Christians in all our endeavors. When the jobs we have taken require extra effort and overtime in order to meet a deadline or some other type of temporary emergency, we should be available for that service. However, if your job continually requires such a total dedication on your part so you never have time for other responsibilities, then you need to do an assessment of your priorities. Or if you find yourself so eager to move ahead that you pour all your energy and vitality into your job, even though it may not be required, that is another signal that you need to stop and take your spiritual pulse and temperature.

One directive given by our Lord clearly defines what our priorities should be: "But seek first His kingdom and His righteousness; and all these things shall be added to you" (Matt. 6:33). The scope of this command, and the promise given with it, are immense. Few Christians have ever dared prove it true in their lives. What does it mean to seek first his kingdom and righteousness? How could any of us hold down everyday secular jobs, which by necessity occupy most of our waking hours, and still claim to seek God's kingdom first?

At first glance, it would seem impossible, wouldn't it? But earlier we talked about God's view of work, and how our jobs can be a vital part of God's plan for our lives. So it is possible to have a job and even career ambitions and still keep our priorities in line with Matthew 6:33. It requires a constant assessment on our part of just what our motives are and where our priorities lie. Is our career drive simply an ego trip, something we're doing to prove that we're capable or to establish our worth? Many times Christians use their jobs as a substitute for finding their fulfillment in the Lord Jesus—the satisfaction and self-esteem that only Jesus can give.

Attitudes toward Money

Another potential trouble area for the person on the success treadmill is the love of money. Success usually brings more money, and that money can get a grip on our lives so fast that we hardly realize it. Unquestionably, all of us work, in part, for money. If our companies did not hand us a paycheck at regular intervals, we'd soon leave the job even if we liked the work.

Is it wrong to work for money? No, and in fact the Bible exhorts us to earn our own way, to be industrious, and not to be dependent on others for our necessities: "But if anyone does not provide for his own, and especially for those of his household, he has denied the faith, and is worse than an unbeliever" (1 Tim. 5:8); "Laziness casts into a deep sleep, And an idle man will suffer hunger" (Prov. 19:15).

Honest work for an honest paycheck is honorable. But how easily money can become our motivation. Not long ago a passage from 1 Timothy 6 really spoke to me on this matter of wanting to make a lot of money.

> There is a real profit, of course. It is peace of heart for those who live as God would have them live. We brought nothing with us when we entered this world and we can be sure we shall take nothing with us when we leave it. Surely then, as far as physical

things are concerned, it is sufficient for us to keep our bodies
fed and clothed. For men who set their hearts on being wealthy
expose themselves to temptation. They fall into a trap and lay
themselves open to all sorts of silly and wicked desires, which
are quite capable of utterly ruining and destroying their souls.
For loving money leads to all kinds of evil, and some men in the
struggle to be rich have lost their faith and caused themselves
untold agonies of mind.

But you, the man of God, keep clear of such things. Set your
heart on integrity, true piety, faithfulness, love, endurance and
gentleness. Fight the worthwhile battle of the faith, keep your
grip on that life eternal to which you have been called, and to
which you boldly professed your loyalty before many witnesses. . . .

Tell those who are rich in this present world not to be contemptuous of others, and not to rest the weight of their confidence on the transitory power of wealth but on the living God,
who generously gives us everything for our enjoyment. Tell them
to do good, to be rich in kindly actions, to be ready to give to
others and to sympathise with those in distress. Their security
should be invested in the life to come, so that they may be sure
of holding a share in the life which is real and permanent.

1 Timothy 6:6–12, 17–19 PHILLIPS

When we begin to set our hearts on more money, a better
position, more status, we're setting ourselves up for spiritual failure. Paul tells young Timothy that we expose ourselves to temptation and various traps. These traps are deceptive and it isn't
difficult to fall into them. What are the traps waiting for those
who set their hearts and ambitions on money and success?

Being contemptuous of others. The first trap is looking down
on others. We begin to think that our money gives us higher
status, more importance, and more validity than other people.
You can probably think of people who have achieved a certain
level of success and have an attitude that says, "I can't waste my
time on less important people anymore."

Becoming contemptuous is an easy trap for people who love
money because they judge people's worth by the amount of
money they earn. And that can happen to any of us. I remem-

ber seeing some statistics about women's salaries a few years ago, and I then became aware of my income in relation to other women. I had never thought about it before, but just seeing those statistics tended to make me think more highly of myself. I was in a higher bracket than I would have guessed, and my opinion of myself increased because of my income.

That's a pretty ridiculous way for a Christian to think. Scripture does not approve of this tendency on our part to judge ourselves and others by the amount of money we make. God certainly doesn't judge us that way. Yet we see it all the time in the working world. More respect is given to the people at the top who earn big money. Their financial success impresses everyone. But remember that while we look on the outward appearance, God looks on the heart. He is no respecter of persons! He could not be less impressed with the dollar amount on our paychecks or in our bank accounts.

Confidence in the power of money. Another trap Paul points out is that people with money put their confidence in its power. Frankly, even people without money do that. We think if we just had a certain income level, things would go well for us. Life's problems would go away. Subtly, we begin to look to money for our security.

I must confess, this area is one of continual learning for me. Since I began The Christian Working Woman radio ministry in 1984, I've seen over and over again how much I have trusted in money in the past and how that has kept me from learning to trust God more completely. Learning to walk by faith and not by sight, for me, centers around this money issue more than any other. And learning not to make all decisions based on money continues to be a challenge for me.

A friend once said to me, "Mary, none of us really wants to be totally dependent on God. We all want our security blankets tucked away in a safe place to get us through any tough spots in our lives." His words were a dagger to my heart, because I had to admit that in this financial area, I could not imagine being without a little money put aside to make sure that I could take care of myself.

Paul warned those who are rich or have a great desire for money not to "rest the weight of their confidence on the transitory power of wealth." How utterly ridiculous for us to put our hope of security in a little—or a large—amount of money. Money is probably the least dependable commodity in the world. Any number of things could happen overnight that would wipe out that money in one blow. Satan has lied to us, and we've come to believe his lie that money can give us security, not to mention happiness and contentment.

Years ago I had an opportunity to purchase my company's stock at reduced rates, and I bought some of that very dependable stock through payroll deductions. The stock was then increasing in value daily, and as one of the ten largest corporations in the world, that stock had perhaps the best reputation of any stock any person could own. I decided never to sell it but to keep it for long-term investment—that nest egg that would always be there, reliable and dependable in case I needed it.

Now, fifteen years later, that stock has plummeted. That wonderful company has come on hard times, and my investment is worth less than I paid for the stock at this point. Often I've smiled as I thought how confident I had always been in that stock holding its value and felt so smug about having some stock there for emergencies or old age. It was a smart investment at the time I made it, but it hasn't proven dependable. Money never is. To try to find our security in money is a foolish thing to do.

That does not mean, of course, that we can be careless and poor stewards of our money or that we should not save and invest for the future. It simply points out that even with sound investments, there is no security in this world's money. Furthermore, there is no real contentment in having money. It doesn't warm your heart or fill up the emptiness inside you.

Real contentment, Paul says, comes only to those who live as God would have them live. This trap of expecting money to bring us security and contentment is so prevalent in our society that for me it almost seems impossible to tear it out by its roots and get it out of my life. But I challenge you, as I'm challenging myself, to prove God true, to change your thinking about money, and to examine where your trust really lies.

Self-centeredness. Another trap we can fall into when we start focusing on earning money is that we become self-centered. Our financial success becomes the focal point of our whole life, and little by little, other things drop off. We become absorbed with amassing riches for ourselves, and that attitude leaves little room for caring for others. Unfortunately, this attitude can creep up on us and take over without our realizing what is happening.

Paul says we are to set our hearts on goodness, Christlikeness, faith, love, patience, and humility. When our minds are focused on earning money or great success, we seldom have time to focus on the virtues that are the fruits of the Holy Spirit operating in our lives.

Think of people you know or have known who set their whole heart on money. Do you really admire them? Were they a pleasure to be with? Were they an encouragement to you? Or were they self-absorbed, frantic, pressurized people who were always in a hurry but never had time for anyone but themselves?

Now think of those you know who set their whole heart on goodness and Christlikeness. I remember a single lady who has now gone home to be with the Lord. She set her whole life on being like Christ. And every day of her life she was an encouragement and a joy to others. She was in our church for many years, and I keep learning of people there whose lives she profoundly affected for the glory of God.

This marvelous woman set her heart on Christlikeness and faith and love and patience and humility, and every year of her life she was more a blessing to others than the year before. She didn't have a lot of money. But her priorities were right on with Scripture and with the exhortation Paul gave to Timothy. She kept her body fed and clothed nicely through the years, but that was never of utmost importance to her. As a result, she was freed from all the cares that the love of money brings, all the worries and fretting and planning and figuring that happens when money is paramount. She was much happier and freer than people I know who have lots and lots of money, and I'm sure she would never have envied their money or possessions.

You know, the love of money is enslaving. When your heart is set on acquiring more and more money, for security or pleasure or prestige, you become a slave and you lose freedom. If you want to know a real freedom of spirit, start breaking the bonds of money in your life.

True, there are Christians who have a great deal of money and who use it to the glory of God. But those people have never loved that money. And if they lost it, it would not destroy them. They know how temporary it is. They have learned the truth of Psalm 62:10: "If riches increase, do not set your heart upon them." As their money has increased, they have simply used it as a gift from God for his glory.

Agur wrote in Proverbs 30:8–9: "Give me neither poverty nor riches; Feed me with the food that is my portion, Lest I be full and deny Thee and say, 'Who is the LORD?' Or lest I be in want and steal, And profane the name of my God."

Jesus told the disciples, "It is easier for a camel to go through the eye of a needle, than for a rich man to enter the kingdom of God" (Matt. 19:24). It is the rare Christian who can handle great financial success well. The traps are many, and the temptations are constant. More often than not, having money ruins a person's commitment to Jesus Christ rather than enhances it. It doesn't have to be that way, but sadly, it often is.

On God's balance sheet, things look a lot different than they do in our checkbooks. He looks on the asset side for goodness, faith, love, patience, humility, Christlikeness. This is what is important to him. So, if you're building your working life around a desire to get ahead and earn lots of money, stop and check it out. The evils that it could lead you into are many. It may be that not having a lot of money is one of the biggest blessings God could give you, because he knows how addicted and enslaved you would become if you had it. Frankly, having a lot of money is something I no longer desire because I fear that I would not be able to handle it well and it would interfere with and perhaps destroy my effectiveness for Jesus Christ. Nothing is worth that.

In the end, how much money you make or have is absolutely unimportant to God. He looks at the set of your heart and searches for those who hunger and thirst for righteousness. He has promised that they will be satisfied. But money will never satisfy anyone.

Again, as Christians in a working world, we have an opportunity to shine as lights in darkness if we exhibit a different attitude about money. If those around us can see that money is not our prime motivator, that we trust in God more than we trust in money, then they have to take notice of that attitude. This is the kind of salt that makes people thirsty for the same water that we have.

What? No Career Ambitions?

What about the women whose ambitions lie in other directions, who have no desire to build outstanding careers or be super businesswomen?

Society's Guilt Trap

One of the negative results of this era of women's rights has been that many women feel guilty because they don't feel a compulsion to climb a career ladder. While many have seen this new environment as challenging and stimulating, a great many others feel caught in the middle. They feel guilty and apologetic about not having career ambitions, as though they have failed as women.

The changes in the nature of the dilemmas facing women has been amazing, even in my short lifetime. When I graduated from high school, not that many years ago, I was expected to want to be a wife and mother. A college education was nice, but no one considered it terribly necessary for a woman. Had I, in the early 1960s, expressed an ambition to become a vice president of a large corporation, I would have received little support or encouragement. I would have been the exception, not the rule, and I would have had an uphill climb because that ambition deviated from the norm.

Just a few short years later, my daughter, having to choose her major in her freshman year at college, felt a great pressure to have definite career ambitions. At the age of eighteen, she felt she was expected to have a plan for her life very clearly in mind, with goals and objectives that would lead her to a successful career. Some of that pressure must have been a result of having a single career mother as a role model for ten years. But such pressure is not unique to my daughter; most girls in high school and college have the subconscious, if not conscious, notion that they must aspire to be more than a housewife, more than a mother. Anything less would denote lack of ambition, lack of intelligence, and a serious deviation from the norm.

Society is beginning to take note of this backlash caused by the feminist movement and the guilt it has placed on many women who do not choose to pursue careers or professions. The pendulum of social change makes great wide sweeps from one side of the spectrum to the other, only briefly touching middle ground as it moves. You may have noticed that lately many television news specials have focused on the woman who has chosen to stay home with her children, forsaking or postponing her career while they are young. Twenty years ago the specials would have highlighted the woman who chose to forgo family pursuits for the corporate world. We've seen, and lived through, dramatic changes in public awareness and expectations for women in the last three decades.

Little wonder that many women have been caught in this pendulum swing, finding it difficult to distinguish their own true ambitions from what is expected of them. As is so often the case, we've again thrown the baby out with the bath water, but this time the analogy is sadly close to reality.

Well, where does that leave us as Christian women if we do not aspire to great career heights yet are a part of the working world? What do we do about these guilt feelings, about the pressure we feel from society to be superwomen, excelling at everything we do?

The lack of career ambitions does not mean the lack of all ambitions or the lack of proper ambitions. A Christian who has no desire to achieve new heights in the working world need feel no guilt for that lack of ambition. Though the system seems to say that all worthy people have ambitions to get ahead in their jobs, that is not a biblical principle, and the Christian working person need not take on the guilt that Satan and his system would lay on us.

If you choose or have chosen to be a wife and mother, and you now have children in your home, it is clear from Scripture that your priority must always be the welfare of your children. If your ambitions are to be the best mom and wife possible, you're in safe spiritual territory. Nothing is more important. So lift your head high when you have an opportunity to tell someone that your top priority is your children and your home, and your career goals are not most important. Never be ashamed of that. It is a wise and intelligent woman who keeps those priorities in line.

Making Quality Your Ambition

The person who does not have career ambitions, though, does need to be careful of certain pitfalls. As long as you work for someone and receive a salary, you are responsible for giving excellent service. While you may not be trying to win any promotions, as a Christian you are commanded to do your work to the best of your ability. Lack of any ambition to advance your career can cause you to lose your drive for excellence. That should never be true of a Christian. Jesus was an extra-miler all the way in everything he did. We must be careful not to damage the testimony of Christ through sloppy or mediocre work.

Think back to or reread our discussion of the parable of the talents from Matthew 25:14–28. I believe this parable also has much to offer us on what Jesus thinks about ambition and success. This parable shows that not all of us are endowed with equal talents and abilities. Have you ever tried to make an objective assessment of whether you are a five-talent, two-talent, or one-talent person—or something in between? Maturity, I am learning, helps us realize, perhaps painfully at first, that certain gifts and abilities are ours within limits and certain others have been denied us altogether. This parable teaches us that the important issue is not how talented or gifted we are. After all, we really had nothing to do with the abundance of our talent or lack of it.

We are not judged by what we start with in the matter of talents. If you do not have a great store of abilities, if you do not have unusual brain power or if you do not naturally possess the mental quickness or agility to move up in the business world, you do not have to feel inferior or abnormal. You will never be judged or condemned by God based on the amount of talent you have to start with.

That alone is a very freeing thought. Regardless of what society may expect, you have one Master who really matters, Jesus Christ; and he tells you clearly in this parable that, for reasons you may not understand, some of us have fewer talents than others. We really need to make an unbiased evaluation of our abilities and accept whatever level is our beginning place. Furthermore, we should not only accept our gifts and limitations but rejoice in them. God has made us the way we are for good and important reasons.

We know that God is not a respecter of persons. Therefore, he does not prefer a five-talent person over a two-talent person, or a two-talent person over a one-talent person. Remember that the two-talent person—who, although he doubled his money, still had less than half of what the five-talent person had—received the same exact commendation from the master. There was no difference in their rewards.

Since the five-talent servant had more to begin with, the master expected him to produce more. The fact that he had much more than the other two was of no special significance to the master. It was what he had done with what he had that was important. Ask God to help you make an honest assessment of your talent and ability level, knowing that the number of talents you have to begin with is not the important issue at all. With that assessment in mind, you need to face an important question: What have you done with the talents given to you?

Notice the outrage of the master when he learns that the one-talent servant has not multiplied his talent. Why would the master be so upset? We're only talking about one small talent here, and from his other two servants he has increased his possessions by seven talents already. Why would the lack of this one talent be so important? This is Jesus' way again of showing us the importance he places on small service. He has told us that a cup of cold water given in his name will be remembered; that the poor widow's mite was a greater gift than all the large offerings of the religious hypocrites; that when we do good to even one person, we do it to him.

Therefore, what the one-talent person did with his talent was just as important to the master as what the five-talent person did. Note what happens to this one-talent servant: what he most dreaded comes upon him—he loses his one talent. Because he did not use it profitably, it was taken away from him and given to a servant who would use it. Burying and hiding a talent will never preserve it. Rather, we can be sure we will lose our talents if we do not use them profitably.

If you find yourself in the working world, for whatever reason, and you are not motivated to go to greater heights in your career, ask yourself if you are using the talents given you to their fullest. Could it be laziness that is keeping you from pushing ahead? Are you squandering abilities that could be used? Remember, God expects us to do our work with the highest possible excellence.

On the other hand, you may have ambitions that are not related to the working world. Your talents and ambitions may be more geared to other types of service. The world may never recognize that as success; but remember, they don't keep God's books. If you are using your talent as God would have it used, whether it furthers your career or not, then you are being a good and faithful servant.

So is it all right not to be ambitious for promotions and titles and places of prominence in the working world? Absolutely. As long as you are certain that you are using your talents to your greatest ability and not hiding them. And as long as you continually bring your priorities before God and keep them in line with his purposes for your life.

Seeing the Invisible

One of my constant prayers is that God will give me eyes to see the invisible. Paul said in 2 Corinthians 4:18 (PHILLIPS) that "we are looking all the time not at the visible things but at the invisible. The visible things are transitory: it is the invisible things that are really permanent." I pray for this because I do not want to be consumed with things that are fleeting and transitory—things that don't last for long.

If you earnestly ask God to give you vision for the invisible, this question of whether or not to be ambitious will be answered. As you see things from his perspective, your priorities will begin to change to his priorities. Spiritually intelligent people, men or women, will see the value of placing their life's ambitions and energies into things that are permanent. When that ambition is uppermost in our lives, all others will find their proper place.

Let's end this chapter right where we started, with Jesus' advice to us from Matthew 6:33: "But seek first His kingdom and His righteousness; and all these things shall be added to you." Those few words spoken by our Master are all we need to know to put our priorities in order for a balanced view of ambition, success, and money.

4
Clothes That
Make the Woman

For those of us in the working world, what we wear takes on even greater importance. We strive for an image, hoping to make the "right" impressions on other people. Society assures us that "clothes make the woman" and urges us to "dress for success."

What about Christian working women? Should we be so concerned about the clothes we wear? We know that clothes do not make a person. Lasting worth and purpose in life only come as we establish a vital relationship with Jesus Christ. God does not evaluate us on how we look; he looks at our hearts and judges us by how we are dressed inwardly. We read in 1 Samuel 16:7: "But the LORD said to Samuel, 'Do not look at his appearance or at the height of his stature, because I have rejected him; for God sees not as man sees, for man looks at the outward appearance, but the LORD looks at the heart.'" Does this mean we should ignore the impact of our clothes? Should we strive to overcome our natural desire to dress beautifully and look good, and instead dress in some different way as Christian women?

Getting Our Priorities in Line

I do not believe we are told to ignore what we wear or to try to "dress down" because we are Christians. First Peter 3:3–4 gives some good insight here:

> And let not your adornment be merely external—braiding the hair, and wearing gold jewelry, or putting on dresses; but let it be the hidden person of the heart, with the imperishable quality of a gentle and quiet spirit, which is precious in the sight of God.

Peter is directing this specifically to women. Isn't it interesting to note that women were as much concerned with clothes and looks then as they are now? Notice that Peter does not admonish them not to adorn the external. He is not forbidding them to try new hairstyles or wear nice clothes and jewelry. What he is saying is, get your priorities in line.

I get the feeling that those women in Peter's day had the same problem many of us have when it comes to clothes. Our natural tendency to dress nicely can easily get out of line, and those clothes can begin to take an undue place of importance and priority in our lives and in our thinking. Though men are not exempt from this problem, women are more susceptible to this unbalanced view of clothes, and we must be very careful to avoid this pitfall.

We can easily fall prey to the idea that our clothes make us more important or of more value. Clothes can start to become substitutes for the really important things in our lives. When I first started my sales career, I became a "clothes horse." There's just no other term for it. I bought clothes to make me feel good; I bought clothes to pick me up when I was down; I bought clothes to impress people; I bought clothes to try to attract men; I bought clothes to bolster my own feelings of self-worth; I bought clothes to overcome my inferiority feelings about my looks. I collected lots of nice clothes for many wrong reasons.

I was looking to clothes to meet my emotional needs. I'm sure you know, without my telling you, that it did not work.

Those emotional needs were only met when, after many years, I truly relinquished control of my life to my Lord and he began to change my emotions and desires—and he met those needs. Gradually, I noticed that my intense desire to buy new clothes began to subside. It was not a conscious decision on my part at first. It was simply that God was convicting me and showing me his priorities for my life. And as I continued to get to know him, I no longer looked to clothes to meet certain needs.

Now, don't misunderstand me. I have not turned against pretty clothes! I'm just as normal as blueberry pie, and you'll find me "oohing and aahing" over nice clothes and pretty jewelry just like anyone else. (In fact, as I write this, I've just received some new clothes for Christmas and can't wait to wear them!) I am still very vulnerable to the desire for clothes, and I think I will always have to work at keeping my priorities straight in this area.

I do, however, sincerely believe it is important for Christians to be careful in their dress and in their appearance, so as not to bring any dishonor to the Lord. Sloppiness and dowdiness are never condoned in God's Word. Peter, remember, did not tell the women to forsake adorning themselves outwardly. Rather, he told them to be sure they understood that external adornment was not nearly as important as internal adornment.

Another benefit of paying appropriate attention and care to how we look is that we become less self-conscious. I've discovered that when I leave the house in the morning feeling that my hair, outfit, and overall appearance is close to optimum, I can forget myself and how I look for the rest of the day. But if, on the other hand, I face a day feeling that my dress is not proper or my hair is not becoming, then all day long I am thinking about myself, running into the ladies' room to try to improve my appearance, fussing with my clothes—in other words, self-absorbed. In that condition I cannot be effective at reaching out to other people and being concerned about their lives because I'm focused too much on myself. For me, that is an important reason to spend the time and effort necessary to look as good as I can.

As Christian women in the working world, it is important that we dress in good taste and in good fashion. Clothes do contribute to others' impressions of us, and we should not ignore that fact. As Paul wrote in 1 Timothy 6:17, God has given us all things to enjoy—and that includes clothes. Our responsibility is to be certain that we do not fix our entire focus on these temporary earthly things.

Our Special Wardrobe

From these passages in 1 Peter and 1 Timothy, it's clear that we should concern ourselves with adorning our inner person more than we do the outer person. There is a very special wardrobe for Christian working women—really for any Christian anywhere. This wardrobe, described in the third chapter of Colossians, will set us apart from others and identify us as women who love and serve Jesus Christ.

> And so, as those who have been chosen of God, holy and beloved, put on a heart of compassion, kindness, humility, gentleness and patience; bearing with one another, and forgiving each other, whoever has a complaint against anyone; just as the Lord forgave you, so also should you. And beyond all these things put on love, which is the perfect bond of unity. And let the peace of Christ rule in your hearts, to which indeed you were called in one body; and be thankful.
>
> verses 12–15

How is this for a wardrobe? Everything is totally within our reach, looks wonderful on all of us, and assures us of being well dressed. These special garments are intended by God for each of us to wear on that inner person; and as Christian working women, we have a unique opportunity to be lights in our working world by learning how to wear these beautiful clothes. Let's look more closely at these inner garments.

Compassion

The first garment is compassion, which can be described as a deep feeling of sharing the suffering of another. You know, it's not hard to find suffering people these days. Mental, physical, and emotional suffering is everywhere, and undoubtedly you have suffering people all around you where you work. Are you aware of their suffering? Do you care?

It seems to me that, all too often, I am quick to blame people and judge them without stopping to think of what they have endured or why they are the way they are. That's especially easy to do on our jobs. We often judge our fellow workers without really understanding their suffering.

Don't you think compassion would look good on your job? If you wear it, you'll give people room to make mistakes. Your prayer list will get longer, because when we care about people, we pray for them. Do you pray for the people you work with? Start praying for them, and watch how much more compassionate you feel toward them. Yes, indeed, we need to wear compassion on our jobs.

Kindness

Kindness is the second garment in the closet of a well-dressed Christian woman. Have you been too busy to wear any kindness lately? Do you take it on and off, depending on your mood or who you're with? Sometimes we are least kind to the people nearest to us. We seem to forget that kindness is important on our jobs—with those people we work with every day. It seems we save our kind behavior for people we don't see very often, as though it were in short supply. God has plenty of it, so wear it to work every day. You'll look terrific!

Humility

Third in this special wardrobe is humility. Society often gives negative connotations to humility, as though it were an undesirable characteristic. It is often viewed as weakness or a Milquetoast personality. Rarely do we associate humility with getting to the top in the business world.

But that's an incorrect assessment. The Bible defines humility as a lack of pride, an awareness of who we are in comparison to who God is. God hates pride. It's at the top of the list of things he hates. If your assessment of yourself is inflated and you have a know-it-all attitude, you're not wearing humility and you're missing an important outfit in your wardrobe.

Gentleness

And then we come to gentleness. I am always overwhelmed with the amazing gentleness of Jesus Christ. Oh, how we need to wear his gentleness to work every day. We need that gentle, quiet spirit which Peter tells us should be our adornment, and which is precious in the sight of God.

Are your words tough or harsh? Do you have a sharp tongue or hasty actions that pierce and hurt people before you realize what you're doing? Then you undoubtedly need to wear more gentleness. Gentle answers turn away anger, we are told in Proverbs 15:1, and a gentle spirit brings peace to chaotic situations. It is a precious garment, and everyone will love it on you!

Patience

The next garment we find in this wardrobe for the inner person is patience. Patience can be defined as the capacity to calmly endure. I have to chuckle when I write that, because if anything is the opposite of what I am, it is calm endurance. This is a really difficult garment for me to wear; it just never seems to fit—always a little too small.

Yet God put it on his list, and he didn't make any exceptions, not even for me. You know, I'm learning that God can make this garment fit me—or rather, make me fit this garment—if I am willing to let him. I've asked him to help me put on patience, and since I've started asking, he has put me into situations that have taught me how to be patient. I'm learning; it fits better now than it did a year ago. If I can wear patience, so can you.

Tolerance

The next garment is "bearing with one another" or tolerance. Tolerance is that beautiful quality of allowing other people to be different from us, even different from what we think they should be, and loving them and appreciating them for what they are. If we wore tolerance to work every day, we wouldn't be upset when people don't do just what we think they should do. We'd allow them more room for error. We'd bend over backwards to understand where they're coming from and give them more time to grow and learn.

How often I expect others to track along with me, to march to the same tune that my band is playing. And God has to remind me that he deals with each of us individually. Just because he is teaching me one lesson doesn't mean that all my friends have to learn it simultaneously! Tolerance is the garment that allows us to "bear with" others, whatever their circumstance.

Forgiveness

The word *forgiveness* itself is beautiful. It brings so much happiness to others when we're able to forgive. God tells us to forgive others as he has forgiven us. That's pretty powerful forgiveness, isn't it? Are you harboring an unforgiving attitude in your heart toward someone? Even if you have been mistreated, you need to put on forgiveness. Even if you haven't been asked to forgive, you need to wear forgiveness. And even if you've forgiven them for the same thing time and again, you need to keep forgiving them.

You'll be amazed to see that in forgiving others, you relieve yourself of an immense burden of bitterness and resentment. Also, you experience God's forgiveness for you in greater measure, so you rid yourself of guilt you've been carrying around. Forgiveness for others reaps enormous benefits for you. Put on forgiveness; it is lovely.

Peace

Peace is the next beautiful garment in God's wardrobe. Are you peaceful? Or do you fret and worry a lot? Is your life frantic? Perfect peace comes by fixing your mind on Jesus Christ. Have you tried on any peace lately? It is the most wonderfully comfortable garment in the whole wardrobe. Once you try it on, you will want to wear it constantly.

Thankfulness

A spirit of thankfulness is absolutely essential in your wardrobe if you want to be a well-dressed Christian working woman. Do you complain a lot about what you don't have or can't do or where you are or who you are? There is usually lots of complaining going on in most any job environment. Are you a part of that complaining? If you wear thankfulness, you won't complain. You'll be too busy counting your blessings. Thankfulness is very attractive. When you wear it you have a certain magnetism; people love to be with you, because it makes you a positive person.

Have you been wearing thankfulness to work? It is a magical garment, because as we learn to give thanks in every situation, we discover that our heaviest burdens grow lighter.

Love

The crowning touch to all the other garments in this unique wardrobe is love. Love is the golden chain of all these virtues, linking the whole wardrobe together into a unified whole. Love covers up blemishes; it fills in the missing gaps and mends the frayed edges. God's love, worn in our hearts, motivates us to want to wear all these garments.

So here it is, God's wardrobe all ready for you to put on: compassion, kindness, humility, gentleness, patience, tolerance, forgiveness, peace, thankfulness, and love. You've heard it said that clothes make the person. Well, whether or not that's true with our outward clothes, it certainly is true with this special wardrobe for our inner persons.

But how do we gather these precious garments into the closet of our heart? It's easy to talk about them, and it's easy for me to admonish you to wear them. But if you're finding that they just don't fit or you don't know how in your everyday situation to be patient or kind or gentle or thankful, then how do you change? How can you put on these beautiful clothes that every Christian working woman should wear?

Worn by Faith

The first thing we must understand is that putting on these garments is not an act of our emotions; it is an act of our will. So often in our Christian walk we want all the feelings in place before we exercise faith. We want to *feel* gentle and humble and peaceful and thankful. And if our feelings aren't working too well on a particular day, then we assume we just can't wear those garments that day because we don't feel them. The sooner we learn that feelings are not a barometer of our spiritual temperature, the sooner we'll be able to take these garments, *by faith*, and wear them.

When you know you're facing a day that will require, for instance, a great deal of patience, keep repeating that you *will* put on patience for that day. Put it on by faith, regardless of whether you feel patient or not. Your feelings will eventually give up and come along with your will, but never mind them. Will to do his will. God will supply the patience when you need it if you don't allow your emotions to destroy your faith. You wear these garments by faith, just as you accepted God's gift of eternal life by faith. The act of your will is your part; God does the rest.

Second, wearing this wardrobe is not a function of our personalities. Many of these inner garments do not come naturally to us. But that does not keep any of us from wearing all of them. We often let ourselves off the hook by saying, "Well, that's just the way I am. I can't be anyone else; I have to be myself." We've been fed this current philosophy of "being your own person" so much that we use it to excuse ourselves from whatever we feel doesn't fit our personalities.

Well, I can't see where God makes any exceptions for personality. He has all the garments you could ever need, and he's ready to impart them to you. Don't let your personality be an excuse for not making God's "Best Dressed List." It is possible—through Christ—for all of us to wear this entire wardrobe.

Needed: An Uncluttered Closet

Maybe one reason you haven't put on all of these garments is that there just is no room in your "closet." Perhaps your wardrobe is cluttered with all kinds of outdated, ugly clothes. In the same third chapter of Colossians we have a list of clothes that we should "put off" (vv. 8–9).

• *Anger.* This is a legitimate reaction to unfair treatment, injustice, and so forth. But if we harbor anger instead of dealing with it properly, then it becomes a part of our wardrobe, and that's when anger becomes a sin. Regardless of whether our anger is justified or not, God tells us to put off anger. It is so unbecoming that if we took a look in the mirror and saw just how that anger looks on us, we'd shed it right away.

• *Wrath.* Add resentment to anger and you have wrath. Resentment is a beastly garment that distorts our thinking, takes over our mind, and keeps us in a state of constant turmoil. Are you resentful and angry toward someone? You may not realize it, but others can see that wrath you are wearing, and it really is the wrong style for you.

• *Malice.* Malice is spitefulness, the desire to see others suffer. It is uglier than even anger or wrath. When we hope that misfortune comes to someone who has made our life tough or unpleasant, that is malice. When we wish our boss would get fired, that is malice. And the world sees that malice we wear. It really is overpowering, and most unattractive.

• *Slander, abusive speech, and lying.* These all go together because they are concerned with what comes out of our mouths. James was really on target when he talked about the tongue as a little flame that can kindle a great fire (see James 3:5). God's wardrobe has no place for this sort of speech coming from our mouths.

Are any of these ugly clothes in your closet? They take up so much room and occupy so much of our time and thoughts that we're left with little room for God's beautiful clothes. Sometimes we wear these unattractive clothes so long that we begin to feel rather comfortable with them. But until we take them

off, we won't know how heavy and confining and unbecoming
they really are. They do not look good on anyone, not even
once in a while.

In Isaiah 61, God says he will give us beauty for ashes, joy
for mourning, and a garment of praise for the spirit of heavi-
ness. What an incredible offer this is from our heavenly Father!
He wants to clean out all those heavy, ugly, dirty clothes now
hanging in our personality wardrobe and replace them with
beauty and joy and praise.

I ask you, in all reasonableness, *How could any straight-
thinking woman refuse his offer?* The only thing required is that
we be willing to exchange our present unsightly wardrobe for
his new garments. We must relinquish the control of our life to
the heavenly Father and be willing to take off our present unattractive clothes, hand them over to him, and accept in exchange
these beautiful inner garments that he desires to give us.

In addition, if we're going to possess these special clothes,
we must prepare a special place for them. It is the closet of prayer,
to which Jesus referred when he was teaching his disciples how
to pray (see Matt. 6:6). You see, our ability to wear these garments is in direct proportion to the quality of our prayer life,
which includes God talking to us through his Word as well as
our petitions to him.

How much time did you spend today praying and meditating on God's Word? Yesterday? This week? Did other less significant, optional activities, such as television or reading the paper
or magazines, occupy more of your time than prayer? God is
showing me that if I really am serious about being his, my prayer
life must be consistent and strong and must occupy the most
important place in my schedule. A prayer closet is essential for
the preservation of this heavenly wardrobe!

Finally, if you really want to be a well-dressed Christian working woman and wear all of these clothes at once (you won't be
overdressed!), I have a suggestion to help you. Every morning
as you get dressed, talk to the Lord, saying something like this:
"Lord, while I'm putting on these necessary outer garments, I
want you to know that I desire to be your best-dressed woman.

I want to put on compassion, kindness, humility, gentleness, patience, tolerance, forgiveness, peace, thankfulness, and love."

Make a list, and tack it on your closet door as a reminder. Memorize the list. And repeat to God every day, using your dressing time as a reminder, that you desire to wear these beautiful clothes he has provided. And by faith, as you put on your outer garments, you are at the same time putting on these inner clothes.

One of Satan's best methods for defeating us is forgetfulness. He'll try to erase your memory and keep you from thinking about God's inner wardrobe. If you don't find a method to remind yourself, you'll be surprised at how other things will crowd your mind, and the day will be over before you've remembered what you should be wearing. This little routine will help you remember.

Recently, a friend of mine took my advice and literally taped this list of inner garments to her mirror. She told me that it was a great help to her in reminding her daily as she dressed of the most important clothes she should be putting on. Why don't you try it on your mirror? See if it helps.

Looking in God's Mirror

In James 1:23–25 we read that a person who simply hears and does nothing about what she hears is like a woman catching the reflection of her own face in a mirror. She sees herself in that moment, but she goes on with whatever she was doing without the slightest recollection of what sort of person she saw in the mirror.

After we dress each day, the last thing we do is check the mirror. To look in the mirror and discover a serious problem with our clothes and then do nothing about the problem is rather ridiculous. The whole purpose of looking into the mirror is to remedy any problem before we go out to face the world.

Have you looked into the mirror lately? What have you been wearing? Do you need a new wardrobe? Are you tired of the drab, weary, heavy clothes in your closet? Don't walk away from

God's mirror without doing something about what you saw. The Bible tells us that those who know to do good and don't do it are sinning (James 4:17).

What happens when you start to take seriously this idea of putting on God's beautiful clothes on a daily basis? Several years ago, as I struggled with lack of patience and kindness and gentleness in my life, I began practicing this principle daily and continue doing it to this very day, consciously putting on patience and kindness and gentleness, along with the other garments.

Then I began to realize what happened. I was keenly aware of my lack of these things during the day. That's the first step. As soon as I would be unkind, my spirit would convict me. God's voice inside me would say, "Kindness just fell off, Mary. Put it back on, please." Then I gradually became aware that I was handling situations and people with more compassion than before. I discovered I really cared about other people's feelings, and I wanted to be kind and gentle. My speech became more tolerant and kind. And to my utter amazement, I discovered that I was becoming patient in situations where before I would have been impossible.

Oh, there is much room left for improvement, but I can testify that it works to put on God's wardrobe every day. And when you go to your job wearing these clothes, you're going to stand out as the best-dressed woman in your working environment. Everyone loves compassion and kindness, gentleness and love, thankfulness and tolerance. They're always in style.

This is not meant to be just a clever way of talking about the fruits of God's Spirit. Rather, it is meant to be a practical way to help you put on these lovely inner garments and watch God transform your life. I challenge you to wear these clothes, by faith, every day and become the best dressed woman on the job.

5

Biblical
Assertiveness

One characteristic today's society considers essential for success is assertiveness. Oftentimes we find ourselves in situations that call for assertiveness, for standing up and being heard, for presenting our arguments forcefully and clearly. What are the biblical guidelines for assertiveness? Are they different for men and women? Is assertiveness on the job different from other types? Those are questions we Christians tend to struggle with.

Another key issue many of us face is trying to distinguish assertive behavior from aggressiveness. What is often admired in men who are outwardly assertive can be criticized in a woman. There's no question that generally men have more latitude in being forthright than women do.

Since *assertive* and *aggressive* are often confused, it will be helpful here to clearly define our terms. *Assertiveness* is characterized by confidence, positiveness, and firmly stating and defending one's rights and opinions. *Aggressiveness*, on the other hand, has a much more negative definition. It is characterized by hostile attacks and forcefulness. It is selfish action that does not care about the good of others.

By differentiating between assertiveness and aggressiveness, we can easily see that aggressive action is inappropriate for any Christian because it does not bear any of the marks of the fruits of the Holy Spirit, particularly kindness, gentleness, love, or peace.

So keep in mind that we're addressing the positive characteristics of assertiveness, not aggressiveness. Now, some personalities are naturally more assertive than others, as is true with all character traits. For those of us who find it easy to be assertive, we need to make certain we don't cross those lines into aggressiveness. For those who don't find assertiveness a natural characteristic, you need to develop that ability for those times when it is needed.

Let's take a look at some women in the Bible to see how they illustrated assertiveness and what we can learn from them.

Biblical Role Models

Deborah

Deborah was a judge over her whole nation, the top ruler in Israel for many years. Talk about a woman ahead of her time—Deborah would be considered very assertive in today's society. Imagine how unique she must have been in her own day, when women's roles were much more limited. God chose her at that point in history to deliver his people from a foreign oppressor. The details of her story are found in Judges 3 and 4. As a judge she undoubtedly was required to demonstrate assertive leadership on a day-to-day basis, but at one point she demonstrated unusual assertiveness as she led her army into battle:

> Now [Deborah] sent and summoned Barak the son of Abinoam from Kedesh-naphtali, and said to him, "Behold, the LORD, the God of Israel, has commanded, 'Go and march to Mount Tabor, and take with you ten thousand men from the sons of Naphtali and from the sons of Zebulun. And I will draw out to you Sisera, the commander of Jabin's army, with his chariots and his many troops to the river Kishon; and I will give him into your hand.'" Then Barak said to her, "If you will go with me, then I will go; but if you will not go with me, I will not go." And she

said, "I will surely go with you; nevertheless, the honor shall not be yours on the journey that you are about to take, for the LORD will sell Sisera into the hands of a woman." Then Deborah arose and went with Barak to Kedesh. And Barak called Zebulun and Naphtali together to Kedesh, and ten thousand men went up with him; Deborah also went up with him.

. . . And Deborah said to Barak, "Arise! For this is the day in which the LORD has given Sisera into your hands; behold, the LORD has gone out before you." So Barak went down from Mount Tabor with ten thousand men following him. And the LORD routed Sisera and all his chariots and all his army, with the edge of the sword before Barak; and Sisera alighted from his chariot and fled away on foot. But Barak pursued the chariots and the army as far as Harosheth-hagoyim, and all the army of Sisera fell by the edge of the sword; not even one was left.

Judges 4:6–10, 14–16

Deborah led her army into a battle that was absolutely doomed for failure by all outward evidence. But she asked God for a miracle, and he delivered her people from the hands of their overwhelming enemy. This most unusual assignment for a woman—to lead an army—required a great deal of assertiveness. Deborah was chosen by God for this leadership role, and she was effectively assertive as a leader. This was part of God's plan. Deborah did not rise to this position by accident. She didn't run for election as our leaders do. She was appointed by God, and she was assertive in a very unusual way.

Esther

Esther also delivered her people from annihilation, but she did it quite differently from Deborah. Because of her great beauty, she was chosen as Persia's queen and used that position to save her people. Her assertiveness was much less obvious than Deborah's, yet it was nonetheless courageous and effective. A passage from the Book of Esther gives us insight into this incredible woman.

Then Esther spoke to Hathach and ordered him to reply to Mordecai: "All the king's servants and the people of the king's

provinces know that for any man or woman who comes to the
king to the inner court who is not summoned, he has but one
law, that he be put to death, unless the king holds out to him
the golden scepter so that he may live. And I have not been summoned to come to the king for these thirty days." And they
related Esther's words to Mordecai.

Then Mordecai told them to reply to Esther, "Do not imagine that you in the king's palace can escape any more than all
the Jews. For if you remain silent at this time, relief and deliv-
erance will arise for the Jews from another place and you and
your father's house will perish. And who knows whether you
have not attained royalty for such a time as this?" Then Esther
told them to reply to Mordecai, "Go, assemble all the Jews who
are found in Susa, and fast for me; do not eat or drink for three
days, night or day. I and my maidens also will fast in the same
way. And thus I will go in to the king, which is not according
to the law; and if I perish, I perish." So Mordecai went away and
did just as Esther had commanded him.

Esther 4:10–17

Esther was the one person who could approach the king and
attempt to save her people, the Jews, from the annihilation
planned by their enemy, Haman. Esther well knew that unless
the king intervened, a person approaching his presence without
his permission would automatically be put to death. But she made
her plans, and without regard for her own life, she approached
the king. Through this assertive action she saved her people.

The Proverbs 31 Woman

No woman could accomplish all that the Proverbs 31 woman
did without being assertive. Her major role was mother and
wife, and she never lost sight of that priority. She was a hard-
working woman who managed her household of many servants.
In addition, she had a real estate business and a manufacturing
business, making and selling linen garments and belts. She dealt
with men in her business transactions, apparently with success.

Sometimes when I think I have a lot to do, I read Proverbs
31. The exceptional woman described there had many roles to

fulfill, and she did so with excellence. You can sense her confidence and firm leadership as she performed her many duties. Being assertive did not conflict with her family duties or ruin her testimony. Her children called her blessed and she was a joy to her husband. She used the talents and abilities God gave her to their fullest.

Lydia

Lydia is a New Testament example of an assertive woman. She was a seller of purple fabrics, which was a prestigious occupation and one rarely held by a woman. It is obvious from her profession and the description of her home that Lydia had achieved considerable success in her business. Through the apostle Paul she came into a personal knowledge of Jesus Christ, and afterward her home became the headquarters for Paul while he was in Philippi.

She brought her whole household to a knowledge of Jesus as Savior, and through her home and her resources the gospel spread to Europe. This was an assertive woman, exhibiting leadership and firm convictions, using what God had given her to be what he wanted her to be. She could not have been as effective as she was in spreading the gospel had she not been assertive. Her story is found in Acts 16.

Guidelines for Assertiveness

What I learn from these women in Scripture is that assertiveness—the confident, positive leadership and ingenuity they demonstrated—is acceptable and commendable for God's women. All of these women were admirable, respected women, operating with God's approval and blessing. Let's look at some specific guidelines we can take from their examples.

Feminine Guidelines

One thing is obvious about these four women in the Bible: They were effectively assertive without trying to behave like men or assume some phony tough exterior. Even when they operated in nontraditional roles, they were able to do so with feminine characteristics suited to their own personalities. Those characteristics varied with these four women as they do with women today. But their assertive roles, given to them by God, did not require any shift from their feminine personalities— from the gentleness of Esther, to the intelligence and wisdom of Deborah, to the elegance of the woman described in Proverbs 31, and the compassionate heart of Lydia. That tells me that I can be all woman and still be assertive. The two are not exclusive. God made each sex unique, with different strengths to complement each other. When we try to eliminate those God-designed differences, we put ourselves at a disadvantage and lose a great deal of our effectiveness. So we don't have to abandon femininity to be assertive, or vice versa.

Are there differences in standards of assertiveness for men and women? I can't find any in the Bible, but I do find differences in standards for the Christian and non-Christian. I believe all Christians, male and female, need a clear understanding of biblical guidelines for assertive behavior that help us know how to make appropriate decisions about our own behavior.

These are only guidelines, which by definition means they are not always black and white and they are not always the same for everyone. Much of the determination is instinctive, and what may be appropriate in one situation would not necessarily be appropriate in another. The guidelines in the next section are presented to help in your own determination of what is or is not within the context of your personality.

Circumstantial and Personality Guidelines

Did you notice that these assertive women in the Bible show a variety of styles? They were not stamped out of the same cookie cutter; each of them had a style and degree of assertiveness in harmony with her circumstances and personality.

Of the four, Deborah was the most assertive, but her circumstances demanded unusually strong leadership. Esther was required to be ingenious and shrewd in asserting herself. Had she approached the king with a strong verbal style of assertiveness, it could have meant her own death as well as the destruction of her people. The Proverbs 31 woman demonstrated a quiet kind of leadership and assertiveness, gently but firmly performing her duties with skill and excellence. Lydia achieved a place of prominence by asserting herself in her business, and then she used that God-given ability to help spread the gospel to people who had never heard.

Our assertiveness should be measured by the context of our circumstances and personalities. We must carefully assess the situations we face and determine what degree of assertiveness is called for and will be effective. To begin with, we must be well aware of our own personalities and what style is appropriate for us.

I remember one particular situation when I was assertive for the right reason, but at the wrong time, in the wrong way, and out of character with my own personality. I was in a meeting with my peers and my manager discussing a proposed change in procedures for my department. I came totally prepared to explain why my proposal was superior to the one currently being considered, which was my manager's idea. I presented my reasons in a very reasonable, documented fashion, not expecting to find any resistance, for it was fairly obvious, at least to me, that this was the best course for the company.

For reasons unknown to me, my proposal struck a very raw nerve and my manager was furious. While he could not deny that my reasoning was correct, he was very angry that I was opposing his suggestion. My peers stated their opinion that my method was the better of the two, and so very grudgingly he decided to accept my proposal. However, in making the concession certain remarks and accusations were made. Mind you, the remarks were inaccurate and unfair, but they were angry words spoken out of turn, and I should have let them go unanswered. Nothing could be gained under the circumstances by any further protestations on my part. But in retributive anger, I made my opposition known in strong terms, which, of course, just made matters worse.

The circumstances did not call for further assertiveness on my part. Furthermore, I have never been particularly effective at retorts and confrontations, especially when they take me by surprise. If I had been quiet at that point, later on I might have had an opportunity to object effectively to the unfair accusations. Certainly my Christian testimony would have been strengthened, for my restrained behavior would have stood in stark contrast to the unrestrained behavior of my manager. I failed to follow the guidelines of keeping within the context of the circumstances and my own personality.

A really good rule of thumb is "When in doubt, don't!" If you have a desire to assert yourself or your ideas in a given situation, but you are unsure if it's the right time or the right place, wait. If assertiveness is appropriate, it will most likely be just as effective tomorrow as today. Waiting will rarely be a wrong course when you are hesitant about the appropriateness of being assertive.

On the other hand, don't hold back for lack of courage when you are convinced that something must be said or done. If it is the right time and the right place, gird up your courage and do what you think is appropriate.

Biblical Guidelines

As I've faced various situations in my career, I've discovered some wonderful guidelines in Scripture to show me how to behave, how assertive to be, and what form that assertiveness should take. I am convinced that none of us will ever encounter a situation that will not fall under a biblical guideline if we truly desire to know what that guideline is. Let me share some of those specific passages that have been of great help to me in this question of assertiveness.

> But the wisdom from above is first pure, then peaceable, gentle, reasonable, full of mercy and good fruits, unwavering, without hypocrisy.
>
> James 3:17

Many times, when facing a decision as to whether or not it was appropriate for me to assert my own ideas, I have used this verse as a testing station. If the wisdom is from God, our motives will be pure, there will be a continuing peace about the situation, our emotions will be under control and therefore gentle, our thinking will be reasonable, and the objectives of our assertive behavior will be for the good of others as well as ourselves. If our proposed action does not pass this fairly stringent test, then it is questionable.

If, however, it does pass this test, we need to act. Remember that even though we believe our proposed action meets these requirements, it may still be a tough thing for us to do. Just because we have a certain amount of apprehension about being assertive does not necessarily signal that it is not God's peaceable wisdom.

There have been times when I've made a decision to take a firm stand on some issue and to assert my own ideas, and when that moment came, there were butterflies in my stomach and the palms of my hands were wet with perspiration. Depending on the significance of the action, and depending on your experience in being assertive, you may also encounter this nervousness at similar moments. That is not necessarily a sign that you don't have God's peace in the matter. His peace is that inner conviction that it is the right thing to do, and if you have that conviction and your idea passes the other tests as well, you don't have to be overly concerned about that natural nervousness.

Let's add to our understanding of assertiveness by looking at a few passages from Proverbs.

> The wise in heart will be called discerning;
> And sweetness of speech increases persuasiveness.
> Proverbs 16:21

The purpose of assertiveness, in many cases, is to be persuasive. We often need to be persuasive in business. But how do we do that? The Bible suggests "sweetness of speech." Does that sound like a principle you would learn in today's M.B.A. courses? It's not exactly "winning through intimidation," is it?

I remember when the Lord first gave me this verse for a particular situation on my job. I felt as though I was being "run over" a bit. As a matter of fact, I was. My suggestions and ideas were more or less dismissed as unimportant. I felt that because I was the only female on the management team, there was an atmosphere of humoring me and tolerating me but never taking me seriously. I kept trying to change the situation by being more forceful. I'm sure my ruffled feathers frequently showed as I argued my positions and tried to get my ideas accepted. Before I realized it, I had assumed an adversary role, and I was getting nowhere. My powers of persuasiveness became less and less effective.

Then I came across this verse one morning in my quiet time with the Lord. "Sweetness of speech increases persuasiveness." Could that be true in this situation? As I meditated on this verse, I realized that "sweetness" here does not mean gushy or coy or emotional; rather, it means easy to swallow. It is analogous to the way we sugarcoat medicine so children will take it. Sweetness makes things palatable. This verse gave me an important guideline to use in my predicament. I gave it thought and prayer, and asked God for wisdom in applying this principle. As soon as I stopped concentrating on the condescending treatment that I felt I was receiving and concentrated instead on finding ways to make my ideas palatable, I started to win. I became more persuasive. By coating my speech and considering the effects of my words, I began little by little to assert my own ideas effectively. Then I was taken more seriously and gradually earned my rightful place as a part of the team.

This is basic psychology that works in any relationship. Try it with your husband or your children, the people who report to you, or your colleagues at work. Discover how sweetness of speech can increase your persuasiveness and make you effectively assertive.

Let's look at another proverb.

> By forbearance a ruler may be persuaded,
> And a soft tongue breaks the bone.
> Proverbs 25:15

Forbearance means tolerance and restraint in the face of provocation. This verse says a ruler—a manager, a boss—can be persuaded through tolerance and restraint.

Would you like to change your manager's mind about something? Are you running into a brick wall? Forbear, be tolerant and restrained, and have a soft tongue, a gentle tongue, even in the face of provocation. Certainly, being able to persuade one's boss is effective assertiveness, and this verse gives us a clear guideline on how to be persuasive with those in authority. It may take a little longer than you would like, but this approach will be successful.

I have a friend who worked for a truly unreasonable manager. She never seemed to be able to get to first base when it came to asserting her ideas. For over two years, while she was praying about the situation and trying to apply this principle of forbearance and tolerance, there seemed to be no evidence that she was making any headway whatsoever with her boss. However, after this long period of seeing no results, she was in a meeting with her boss and out of the blue he told her that he had great respect and admiration for her and expressed a desire that he could be more like she was. It really took her by surprise, because she had not been able to see that her tolerance in the situation was having any effect whatsoever. But this manager was testing her and watching her all that time, and he admitted that her behavior and lifestyle had made an indelible impression on him.

God has a right to use situations like this in our lives to bring glory to his name, and we may not even be aware that he is doing it. Forbearance is waiting on the Lord, patiently giving him time to accomplish his purposes.

Here is another valuable piece of wisdom.

> Pride goes before destruction,
> And a haughty spirit before stumbling.
> Proverbs 16:18

Assertiveness, out of control, can easily take on a know-it-all attitude with an arrogant and haughty spirit. Often, a little success will go to our heads. When we have been effectively assertive in one instance, we start to think that we have the tiger by the tail, and we take on a prideful attitude. When this happens you can be sure of one thing: Stumbling and failure are right around the corner. Pride is a hideous sin that plagues us most when we have had a measure of success. I often remind myself that pride is at the top of the list of the things God hates most. We must carefully monitor our thoughts and attitudes to be sure that pride does not creep in.

These are a few of the many verses that give us guidelines in asserting ourselves on the job. They are God's principles of behavior, and they hold true for all Christians, male or female. They are God's psychology, and since he is our Creator, he understands how to deal with human nature better than anyone else.

Our responsibility remains very simple, though not always easy, and that is to obey without hesitation. Jesus said that those who love him keep his commandments (John 15:14). Our obedience is the measure of our love for him.

Just because these principles are not compatible with most of today's accepted rules does not mean they are not effective. This world has not outgrown God's principles. It is true that God's methods will often be at variance with the world's. But we will find as we apply them that they really work, while the world's methods lead us to sure defeat.

Perhaps you are asking, "Then how do we account for all the successful people in the business world who are not Christians?" Well, some of them do follow God's principles, and even though they are not consciously serving God, God still honors his principles. There are many honest, moral people who will enjoy God's blessing on their efforts because of their commitment to right thinking and acting.

Second, when we speak of success we must think long-term. It is possible to win through intimidation, to be dishonest and come out ahead, to climb the ladder on the backs of other people, to play political games and gain promotions thereby, to compromise moral standards and have temporary success. People do it all the time. But in the winning, they create many enemies and problems that come back to haunt them later on. What you sow you reap; it is a basic principle that cannot be escaped. We may not always be around for the harvest; it may be eternity before some people reap what they have sown, both good and bad. But you can be absolutely certain that harvest time will come.

What I have noticed is that more often than not people who disregard God's principles have only short-term success. And even that success brings them no peace or satisfaction. God's ways are peaceable, we can live with them easily. They won't keep us awake at night wondering how to cover our tracks.

A Gentle and Quiet Spirit

Before moving on with this subject of assertiveness, we should address the Scripture reference that often comes up when we speak of women's behavior.

In the same way, you wives, be submissive to your own husbands so that even if any of them are disobedient to the word, they may be won without a word by the behavior of their wives, as they observe your chaste and respectful behavior. And let not your adornment be merely external—braiding the hair, and wearing gold jewelry, or putting on dresses; but let it be the hidden person of the heart, with the imperishable quality of a gentle and quiet spirit, which is precious in the sight of God.

1 Peter 3:1–4

This passage is frequently confusing to women, particularly those in leadership roles. Maybe you, too, have wondered if this passage means that women are to be seen and not heard. Does the gentle and quiet spirit spoken of here prevent us from being assertive? Let's dig more deeply into the meaning of this verse.

This passage is directed to wives, particularly those who are married to unbelievers. Peter gives them a principle for winning their husbands to Christ. It is a principle that works in any close relationship when an unbeliever is united to a believer.

What is it about a Christian that is inviting to a non-Christian? Is it a constant barrage of words and Bible verses and condemnation and judgment? Obviously not. That kind of behavior doesn't attract anyone to anything. But if we are especially close to a non-Christian—say a husband, a brother or sister, a parent, even a roommate or a coworker—we can easily become lecturers and judges and critics. I think Peter's message has a much broader meaning for us, which is: if we are trying to win someone to Jesus Christ, someone who is very close to us, the best thing we can do is let him or her see in our lives that Christianity works. Peter says that "without a word" they may be won.

Our Lord's Assertiveness

Peter tells us that a quiet and gentle spirit is precious in the sight of God. This kind of attitude is not intended to be limited to women only. We know that because the same words were used by our Lord to describe his own spirit:

> Come to Me, all who are weary and heavy-laden, and I will give you rest. Take My yoke upon you, and learn from Me, for I am gentle and humble in heart; and you shall find rest for your souls. For My yoke is easy, and My load is light.
>
> Matthew 11:28–30

We can easily understand why this gentle spirit is so precious to God, since it was the spirit of his beloved Son. Men, as well as women, need to have a gentle and quiet spirit.

Jesus frequently treated people with gentleness and compassion when others were condemning and intolerant. For example, the woman taken in adultery, the Samaritan woman he found at the well, Zacchaeus the hated tax collector, the blind man who wouldn't be silenced until Jesus healed him, the woman who touched his garment, the hungry crowds who had come to hear him teach—the list is endless.

Then, during his trials, Jesus did something we would never expect—he refused to defend himself against all false accusations. Every time I read those passages in John 18 and 19 and Matthew 27, I want to cry out, "Lord, don't let them say those things about you. Don't let them accuse you falsely. Defend yourself!" But Jesus knew this was his destiny; it was necessary, and it was his Father's will. So he refused to demand his rights and instead never uttered a word.

His silence, however, was not an indication of weakness. He was in no way intimidated by his accusers. His refusal to assert himself in this instance was a result of his choice to do the Father's will. He had settled that issue the night before in Gethsemane, when in agony he affirmed to his Father "Not My will, but Thine be done" (Luke 22:42).

Verbal assertiveness is not the only avenue through which we can be strong. In fact, it is often the easy way out for us. Gentleness is much more demanding and requires greater discipline and self-control. In most cases, gentleness will get us further than a verbal, outwardly assertive attitude. Remember, gentleness is not weak; rather, it is very strong.

A gentle and quiet spirit does not prevent us from being assertive. Jesus was frequently bold and assertive in his words and actions. Think of how he threw the money changers out of the temple when they were misusing God's house for their own personal gain. Without hesitation he asserted his authority and literally ran them out (see Matt. 21:12–13). The Gospels also tell us of many of his confrontations with the religious hypocrites. He wasted no words in condemning them and telling them in no uncertain terms just what he thought about them. Matthew 23 reveals his strong words to the scribes and Pharisees. He pronounces judgment on them, calls them hypocrites, blind guides, fools, sons of murderers, and serpents. His gentle and quiet spirit was appropriately assertive when the circumstances called for it, and that assertiveness was in keeping with his own personality.

Jesus is our supreme example for appropriate assertiveness. He had the perfect balance in his life and knew when to be vocal and when to be silent.

The Right Motivation

An important characteristic of Jesus' assertiveness is that his motivation transcended his own individual rights. Though often falsely accused and maligned, he never defended himself or his own reputation. He stood against evil and injustice; he condemned hypocrisy and evil. But never did he become assertive in defense of his own personal rights. Time and again he asserted his authority, but never strictly for his own personal gain.

When you think of the four women we cited earlier, you can say the same thing about them. Their assertiveness was never just on their own behalf. Certainly they benefited by their assertive actions. Deborah saved her people from being taken captive by Sisera, and in doing so she saved herself. Esther prevented the annihilation of the Jews, including herself. The Proverbs 31 woman provided for herself as well as for her household. While Lydia advanced the gospel of Jesus Christ through the resources she had earned in her profession, she also enjoyed those resources herself. It is not wrong to be assertive for a cause that will benefit us. But if our only objective is to defend ourselves or demand our personal rights, without regard for the effect on our testimony or on others, we are on thin ice spiritually.

Often, assertiveness in the business world is used simply to demand one's rights. People readily become aggressive when they think their personal rights are being violated. I read an advice column in a secular magazine for working women. It seems that a new manager had come on the scene and changed all the rules for the particular woman who had written for advice. Money and privileges given her by her former boss were abruptly taken away and promises broken. The advice given to her by a leading business consultant and job counselor consisted of two pages of how to strike back at that company, how to outwit that manager, how to get revenge for the wrong done to her, how to cause legal problems for the parent company, and how to take advantage of them to the fullest extent.

As I read this article, my natural tendency was to react, "Right! Fight for what is yours and get your pound of flesh." That is what our human nature will always lead us to do, for we are born with self on the throne of our lives. But I realized that if this lady follows the advice given, many other people will suffer—customers, other employees, and other managers. And there was no guarantee that, by inflicting all this suffering, this woman would have achieved anything at all for herself except vengeance.

In contrast, I recall a woman we featured in one of our newsletters. After long and loyal service to her large corporation and with many positive affirmations of her good work, she was falsely accused of poor work and put on probation. It was an attempt to thin the ranks at this company, which was downsizing by forcing people out. She assertively defended herself in appropriate ways, but nothing she said or did made any difference.

She then contacted an attorney and began legal proceedings, which caused even more animosity on the part of her management. She was at the point where she needed to move forward in her legal suit, but she had no peace about it. Finally, she came before the Lord in prayer, telling him that if she dropped the legal proceedings, she would have no way of getting her revenge and the men who were doing this injustice could very well walk away scot-free. By verbalizing how she felt to the Lord, she realized that her motive was not, in fact, a desire for justice, but vengeance.

She searched the Bible for instances in which the Lord redeemed his people in battle. Each time the only requirement was obedience, and it was the Lord's job to win the war. She decided she must simply trust God and let him fight for her, so she told her attorney to drop all legal action. She said, "This was a surrender, and with surrender there is death to self. I felt that death, but with it was the sweet joy of obedience. It also allowed me to forgive, which I couldn't have done had I taken them to court. In fact, I realized the only way to forgive them was to place it in God's hands, even if that meant they would be 'let off the hook.'"

She returned to work with contentment and joy, still not knowing what was going to happen to her. Almost immediately there was a change in her supervisor's response toward her. Day by day she saw changes in his attitude, and eventually he gave her a very positive appraisal. She says, "I believed the Scripture that says that the king's heart is like rivers of water in the Lord's hands [Prov. 21:1]. God changed the hearts of my management. All I had to do was be obedient to the Lord."

The Guiding Principle

In summary, as Christians we have an overriding principle under which we operate. Our actions must always bring glory to God. There are times when assertiveness is totally compatible with that objective. As we have already seen, Jesus was frequently assertive in his actions and words. But there are times in our business lives when it will not be appropriate for us to be assertive, even if the cause is right. There are times when we must back away from defending our rights and let God be our defense.

I am well aware of how difficult it is to let go of a situation where we feel we've been treated unjustly and allow God to be our defense and settle the accounts. But if we could just practice that principle and let God have a chance to prove how beautifully it works, we would be amazed to see that God's defense is far better than our own.

This does not correlate with society's current passion for standing up for your rights, I know. And I am not saying that we should not take stands against injustice or prejudice or unfair treatment, whether it is directed toward us or toward others. But if our form of assertiveness is simply to fight for our own personal rights and our own personal gains, then it does not conform to the example given us by our Lord.

A good question to ask yourself is: Would Jesus be assertive here? Remember his kind of assertiveness was against evil and for the good of others. If we Christian working women could start to apply this principle on our jobs, our colleagues would soon have to take notice. An assertiveness that is controlled by these principles is so different from what people expect, they will not be able to avoid the light they see in us, and the saltiness of our lives will make them thirsty.

And that's the bottom line: How can we be salt and light in this world where we work? That's what counts for eternity. Far more important than establishing new roles and blazing new frontiers for women at work is our directive to be witnesses in a dark and tasteless world.

If this sounds difficult or too idealistic to you, I would encourage you to rethink your reaction. It may be difficult, but it is so much easier than constantly standing vigil over your own rights and interests. And if it seems idealistic, it's only because so few Christians have ever dared to apply God's principles in the workplace.

Why don't we break some new ground and determine to be assertive as Jesus would be? As one woman whose natural tendency is to fight hard for her own rights and for fair treatment, I can tell you that his way is so much better. It is peaceable and pure, and far more effective than the world's methods.

6

Loving
the People
We Don't Like

Getting along with other people—whether they're family or friends, whether the relationship is of our choosing or one we cannot escape, whether it is a short- or long-term association—is always a challenge. But in learning to get along with other people, we can learn a great deal about ourselves and grow in the process. Relationships are often God's sandpaper that he uses to smooth the rough edges in our lives.

In the working world, we usually have little to say about who our coworkers will be. We find we are in the company of people who don't think as we do, who don't have the same values we do, who don't have lifestyles similar to ours. They are people we would never choose as friends, yet in our jobs we are forced to spend many hours each week in close association with them. If we were candid, we would probably admit that we frequently work with people we do not really like. It is an environment ready-made for problems in getting along with others.

Liking or Loving?

What can we do as Christians when we find ourselves in this kind of situation? How can we get along with people we don't really like? The first thing to understand is that running into people you don't like is unavoidable. There is no reason to feel guilty just because you do not like certain persons. It's okay! I'm sure there were people Jesus did not like. Read what he said to the religious hypocrites of his day:

> You blind guides, who strain out a gnat and swallow a camel!
>
> Woe to you, scribes and Pharisees, hypocrites! For you clean the outside of the cup and of the dish, but inside they are full of robbery and self-indulgence. You blind Pharisee, first clean the inside of the cup and of the dish, so that the outside of it may become clean also.
>
> Woe to you, scribes and Pharisees, hypocrites! For you are like whitewashed tombs which on the outside appear beautiful, but inside they are full of dead men's bones and all uncleanness. Even so you too outwardly appear righteous to men, but inwardly you are full of hypocrisy and lawlessness.
>
> Matthew 23:24–28

And that's not all he said. The entire twenty-third chapter of Matthew is similar in tone. Frankly, I cannot imagine any stronger words against someone's character than these words of Jesus. Now, could you realistically say that Jesus liked these people?

I think it is clear that even Christians are allowed to have people in their lives they do not like. I know of no scriptural directive that commands us to like everyone. But I know many verses that tell us to love other people. Let me highlight a few.

> And this commandment we have from Him, that the one who loves God should love his brother also.
>
> 1 John 4:21

> The one who does not love does not know God, for God is love.
>
> 1 John 4:8

Love your enemies. . . . If you love those who love you, what
credit is that to you? For even sinners love those who love them.

Luke 6:35a, 32

You shall love your neighbor as yourself.

Leviticus 19:18

These are just a few of the many verses that give us a clear directive to love people—all people, friends, neighbors, enemies—
and yes, even the people we work with.

Though we can conclude that there probably were people
Jesus did not like during his earthly ministry, we also know that
he loved those people. He died for those scribes and Pharisees,
just as much as he died for his disciples. And because he died
for them, we know he loved them. So, though we are not
required to like everyone we know, we are required by Scripture to love them.

When you run into these unlikable people, though, you feel
as if you've hit the spiritual brick wall. Since we cannot like them,
we usually conclude that we cannot love them either. Our thinking is that we like people before we love them. We think of
"like" as the first step of "love." With that reasoning, the command of Scripture to love everyone seems impossible.

However, I have good news for all of us. We don't have to
like someone to love them. To like someone means that we admire
them, enjoy them, want to be like them, and benefit greatly from
their presence in our life. Webster defines *like* as to "feel attraction toward or take pleasure in" someone. I believe "liking"
someone is a feeling. You can't like someone without having
good feelings about them. And since God would never require
of us something we could not do, he has given us power as Christians through the Holy Spirit to love those whom we do not like.

Defining Love

First, let's clarify the type of love we're talking about. There
are three Greek words that are all translated "love":

- *Eros* is love between sexes.
- *Philos* is love between friends and family.
- *Agape* is the kind of love that characterizes God. This is the love that loves because its own inherent nature is to love. That's why the Bible says, "God is love." Love is his nature.

The kind of love we need in order to love people we don't like is agape love. And actually, if the other two types of love—eros and philos—do not at some point mature into agape love, they will eventually fall apart. Agape love is the kind that lasts over the long haul. It's the quality of love that makes marriages really work and friendships last forever. So keep in mind that we're talking about agape love.

Agape love is not a feeling. Though we may experience nice, warm feelings as a result of agape love, it is in no way dependent on how we feel. It does not depend on how others feel about us. We can love with agape love whether the feelings are present or absent, whether they are good or bad.

Agape love is an action. When this type of love is described in Scripture, it is always described as an action, not a feeling. The Bible tells us that we know that God loves us because he sent his Son into the world to redeem us (John 3:16). We know that Jesus loves us because he gave his life for us. The Bible says, "Greater love has no one than this, that one lay down his life for his friends" (John 15:13). And God says that he will know that we love him if we keep his commandments (John 14:15).

This really is good news, because it tells me that I can love people toward whom I do not necessarily have good feelings. I can love people toward whom I have no feelings at all. Since love is an action, not a feeling, I can obey God's command to love everyone.

Love Actions

Since love is an action, how does love act? First Corinthians 13 is a good place to look for a practical description of love actions.

- *Patience.* When you act with patience toward someone, you are loving them. Keep in mind that love is not a feeling, so we don't have to feel patient. If you act patiently, whether you feel patient or not, you are showing agape love.

• *Kindness.* Kind words are love actions. You can say something kind, even if you might feel like being sarcastic or cutting. You can act in kindness toward other people, regardless of whether you like them or not.

• *Lack of jealousy.* When you refuse to behave jealously or possessively, you are showing love.

• *Courtesy.* Just plain courtesy is a love action. How often we forget good manners, like not interrupting others when they're talking and holding the door for those behind us.

• *Unselfishness.* Agape love acts in an unselfish manner, without pursuing selfish advantage or trampling over others in trying to get what you want.

• *Endurance.* When others have given up and left, agape love will still be there hanging in with someone, perhaps listening to a seemingly endless stream of problems.

These are just a few of the many love actions available to us. Others are gentleness, compassion, tolerance, all from our Christian "wardrobe."

Perhaps you are thinking, "If I act with love toward someone when I don't feel like doing it, isn't that hypocritical?" No, I don't think so, because God's love to us is not based on our "lovableness." Remember, Jesus loved those very same scribes and Pharisees whom he so strongly denounced. He may be, and I'm sure often is, displeased with us as individuals, yet his love is constant. Therefore, he does not require of us to have good feelings toward everyone, but rather to act in love toward everyone.

Write it on a piece of paper and tape it to your mirror, your desk, over your sink, wherever you will see it often: "Love is not a feeling; love is an action!"

Developing Love Actions

How do we get these love actions going in our lives? It's one thing to know we should love people we don't like. It's another

thing to make it happen. Paul said in his letter to the Romans
that the Holy Spirit, who was given to us, has poured out the
love of God within our hearts (Rom. 5:5). That's where it starts,
when we accept God's love and the Holy Spirit starts spreading it all through our inner selves.

Think about God's love for you. John wrote: "To us, the
greatest demonstration of God's love for us has been his send-
ing his only Son into the world to give us life through him. We
see real love, not in the fact that we loved God, but that he loved
us and sent his Son to make personal atonement for our sins"
(1 John 4:9–10 PHILLIPS).

And remember, God loves those people you don't like just as
much as he loves you. Let God's love pour all over you and fill you.
Remember how he loves you, even when you're not very lov-
able. That's the beginning of learning how to love other people.

A prerequisite to developing love actions toward these unlikable people in your life is to change your thinking. There's no
way you can keep on thinking of how irritating they are or how
thoughtless, or annoying, and then turn around and have love
actions toward them. What you think will come out in your
actions.

So, remember God's love for you, change your thinking
about these unlikable people in your life, and then pray for them.
Sincerely, regularly pray for their welfare. As much as you know
about them, pray in detail for them. Ask God to show you what
love actions to take toward them. Jesus taught us to pray for
our enemies and those who despitefully use us. As you pray
about these people you don't like, ask God for wisdom in knowing which love actions are appropriate for each person. Does
one require a lot of patience? Does one require compassion or
endurance? When you have discerned the need, set your will to
act with those love actions toward those people.

The Amazing Results

I want to tell you what happens when you start acting with
love toward people you don't like. First of all, you lose guilt—

the guilt you experience when you don't treat certain people very nicely. Second, your love actions will have an effect in most cases. That should not be the reason for your love, but it nevertheless may well bring about a change in the person to whom your actions are directed. And third, you're going to get to know God's love for you in a completely new way. When you start to show agape love toward others, then God's agape love for you will become so much more real and precious.

Learning to love people you don't really like is the key to getting along with your coworkers. Instead of trying to change them, which almost never happens, change yourself instead. Rather than concentrating on how difficult they are, concentrate on how you can find ways to love them, even though you don't like them.

Of course, it's never fully perfected, never once and for all. It is an every-day commitment. But you don't want to miss this wonderful experience of loving people you don't like. Are you willing to try? Even with those people you work with who drive you crazy? You could make a covenant with God today that you are going to begin the process and discover what it really means to show God's love to others.

7

The Impossible
Boss

"He's absolutely impossible. He has no integrity, lies continually, is deceitful and cruel."

"She's absolutely impossible. She treats people like dirt, always making others look bad in front of other people."

"He's absolutely impossible. He never listens to anyone else, thinks he knows everything, and behaves like a dictator."

"She's absolutely impossible. She doesn't know what she's doing and won't admit it."

"He's absolutely impossible. He can't make a decision, never gets anything done, and blames all the problems on me."

"IMPOSSIBLE! My boss is impossible!"

How many times have you heard something like that? How many times have you said it yourself? If you haven't run into the impossible boss yet in your career, it's highly likely that you will at some time or another. Few of us escape the experience of learning to cope with a difficult boss.

What is particularly difficult about having such managers is that we cannot avoid them, and it behooves *us* to get along with *them*. When our peers or coworkers are difficult, there is usually some way of escaping them or avoiding them or telling them to "cool it." But when it comes to our managers, we are usually stuck. It seems like the only way out is to quit, find a new position in the company, or hang in there until the boss moves on.

Someone gave me some good advice early in my career, and that was "It's your job to get along with the boss, not his or her job to get along with you." That may sound unfair, but it is very realistic, and it is good advice for anyone pursuing a career. From personal experience, however, I can tell you that it can be difficult. I, for one, did not always succeed throughout my career at getting along with my managers.

Some Simple Strategies for Surviving

I keep a journal, what I call a spiritual journal, which is simply a blank book where I write what God is teaching me through his Word. I would encourage you to start this practice too if you haven't already. It has proven to be a great blessing in my life to go back and read where I've been and how God has led me. Also, it captures the lessons God teaches me—things I might otherwise forget.

It is from that journal that I can recall so clearly a time in my career when I thought I just could not work any longer for my current boss. The words written in my journal were "I can't take any more." I'm sure there are many of you who've been at that exact spot with your boss—or maybe you are now. You know what I'm talking about. My tolerance and patience were gone. I had endured what seemed to me inordinate amounts of unreasonable and unkind treatment. Frustration reigned supreme in my life. My manager's style was to manage through intimidation and humiliation, and I was not at all competent or experienced in handling it.

As a result of the frustration, I frequently handled confrontations poorly, making matters worse. At one point I wrote in my journal, "Lord, I know that I didn't handle that encounter with my boss very well yesterday." Like the psalmist, I wanted to say, "O, that I had wings like a dove! I would fly away and be at rest. Behold, I would wander far away" (Ps. 55:6–7a).

Yes, I wanted to walk out and never go back to that job. Maybe that's where you are today. Let me encourage you to read Psalm 55. You will appreciate the openness of David in expressing the feelings that are so similar to yours. Somehow, it always helps to know someone else has had the same problem you have.

And here in Psalm 55 he is experiencing the same kind of frustration that you are experiencing if you really want to run away, from your job or anything else. Let's see what we can learn from him.

Learning to Call on God

David does not remain in that depressed, desperate state. In verse 16 of Psalm 55, he comes to an important decision: "As for me, I shall call upon God, and the Lord will save me." And again in verse 18: "He will redeem my soul in peace from the battle which is against me."

David begins to think about something besides his own predicament. He gets his eyes and his thoughts on God and determines that he will call upon God to save him. He further states his conviction that God will deliver him in peace. As a result of this experience, David gives us one of his most beautiful words of advice and comfort: "Cast your burden upon the LORD, and He will sustain you; He will never allow the righteous to be shaken" (v. 22). His psalm ends simply, "But I will trust in Thee."

This is the first step in dealing with an impossible boss: Call upon the Lord. We must focus our eyes on our God, not on our boss. This is an act of our will, and it takes much time in prayer and in God's Word. It is very important that we openly pray about our impossible boss and ask God to give us his view of this whole situation.

As you read Psalm 55, meditate on it carefully. Make sure you are willing to look at the situation through God's eyes. And cast your burden on the Lord; he'll keep you going. He'll keep you from quitting or running away. He will never allow his righteous child to be shaken.

Checking for Self-Pity

The second thing God pointed out to me was that my whole attitude was self-centered and self-pitying. All my thoughts were "I can't take this," "This isn't fair to *me*," "I don't have to endure this kind of treatment." I realized I had to start thinking differently. God said to me, "Mary, it really doesn't matter what inconvenience or uncomfortableness or frustration this situation causes you! That is not what is at issue here." My reply was, "Sure seems that way to me, Lord!" I didn't have very much perspective. (Don't be surprised to find you lack perspective when you're in the midst of this kind of situation. God knows how easily we get caught up in the "me" part of it all. We need to allow him to change our perspective.)

When we can see that there is an eternal purpose in what we're going through, things will look different to us. God clearly showed me the need to change my thinking from "Poor me—what can be done to deliver me from this terrible spot?" to "How can God be glorified in this situation? What are his purposes for putting me in this place?" When I finally could look at it that way, much of the frustration left immediately.

Eternal viewpoints are wonderful, because they deliver us from the bondage of the here and now. The trouble often is that we are so caught up in our self-pity that we really don't want to give it up. Even though relinquishing it is our doorway to freedom from frustration, we've become so accustomed to being wrapped up in it that it is almost strangely comforting. I've noticed that tendency in myself and in others. Self-pity can hold a strange attraction for us.

Maybe you need an eternal viewpoint in your situation. Perhaps you've just become consumed, as I was, with what it was doing to you, and you need instead to ask God about his purpose. And you ask, not in a demanding way, but in submission. "Lord, I submit to your will. What would you have me learn and how can you be glorified?" That's an important step to take in dealing with an impossible boss.

Tolerance

Then God showed me some other passages in Scripture that shed more light on dealing with a difficult boss. Proverbs 25:15 says: "By forbearance a ruler may be persuaded, and a soft tongue breaks the bone." Forbearance means tolerance or length of anger. Even if your anger is justified in your particular situation, you need to lengthen it. Stretch it out; don't have a short fuse. And, most importantly, keep a soft tongue. With forbearance and a soft tongue, a ruler can be persuaded. If you want to change your boss's behavior toward you, try God's principles. They are very clearly set forth here. Be tolerant and speak with gentleness and kindness. And watch what happens.

Discernment and Persuasiveness

Another helpful verse is Proverbs 16:21: "The wise in heart will be called discerning, and sweetness of speech increases persuasiveness." Two useful traits in dealing with an impossible boss are discernment and persuasiveness. Discernment gives us the ability to know what to say and when, to see subtleties we might have missed before, to distinguish between good and bad ideas. And we certainly could use a little persuasiveness in these situations, to be convincing and influential with that difficult manager.

This Scripture tells us that the wise in heart are discerning. What does it mean to be wise in heart? We are told in 1 Corinthians 1:24 that Christ is the wisdom of God. In order to be truly wise in heart, we must have Christ and the Spirit of Christ dwelling within us. Without him there is no real wisdom. So, we need to constantly be learning more of Jesus, and that comes from the Word of God. We have to be saturated with Jesus in order to be wise in heart.

Also, in James 3:17 we read that "the wisdom from above is first pure, then peaceable, gentle, reasonable, full of mercy and good fruits, unwavering, without hypocrisy." Try testing your ideas and attitudes toward your boss by these criteria; that's the kind of wisdom that will make us discerning.

Then, once again, we must check out our speech if we want to be persuasive. Tough talk, belligerent words, hostile confrontations, and contentiousness will not increase our persuasiveness. But words that are easy to swallow, palatable, sweet words, these will make us much more persuasive in dealing with our management.

Putting Aside Malice

Malice is the desire to see something bad happen to someone. Oh, how easy it is to fall into that trap when we are working for difficult managers. Since we cannot usually express our displeasure to them, we can let our imagination run wild. We wish they would make a big mistake and their boss would catch them. We wish they would get fired. We wish higher management would see how bad they are. Several verses warn us about malice:

> But now you also, put them all aside: anger, wrath, malice, slander, and abusive speech from your mouth.
>
> Colossians 3:8

> Therefore, putting aside all malice and all guile and hypocrisy and envy and all slander.
>
> 1 Peter 2:1

> Let all bitterness and wrath and anger and clamor and slander be put away from you, along with all malice.
>
> Ephesians 4:31

It is clear from these passages that malice has to be dealt with decisively. It is easy to have malicious thoughts without realizing how sinful and harmful they are. Paul and Peter give us strong admonitions to get rid of malice—put it aside, take it off. Again, by an act of our will, not our emotions. We have to take off that malice toward our difficult boss. Whether he or she ever changes, we must obey God. It is clear that there is no place in a Christian's life for malice.

Learning to Endure Wrong Treatment

The Bible has much to say about how employees should treat their managers and how managers should treat their employees, and the following is a classic passage.

> Servants, be submissive to your masters with all respect, not only to those who are good and gentle, but also to those who are unreasonable. For this finds favor, if for the sake of conscience toward God a man bears up under sorrows when suffering unjustly. For what credit is there if, when you sin and are harshly treated, you endure it with patience? But if when you do what is right and suffer for it you patiently endure it, this finds favor with God. For you have been called for this purpose, since Christ also suffered for you, leaving you an example for you to follow in His steps, who committed no sin, nor was any deceit found in His mouth; and while being reviled, He did not revile in return; while suffering, He uttered no threats, but kept entrusting Himself to Him who judges righteously; and He Himself bore our sins in His body on the cross, that we might die to sin and live to righteousness; for by His wounds you were healed.
>
> 1 Peter 2:18–24

Yielding to authority. It is really important that all of us employees understand and obey this principle given to us by Peter. First, he tells us we are to submit to our masters with all respect—and not just to the nice ones but also to those who are unreasonable.

How do we do that? Submit means to yield to the authority of another; to be obedient. That's the first step: yield to the authority of your boss, with respect. I can hear some of you asking, "How can you act with respect toward someone whom you really do not respect?" The same way you can love someone you don't like, as we discussed in chapter 6.

Respect means, in addition to other things, to treat with consideration. And you can do that even if your feelings are contrary. Remember, we cannot be run by our emotions; that will get us into trouble every time. We must set our will to do what is right, and let the emotions go. You must will to respect that unreasonable boss and to be obedient to him or her.

Romans 13:1–2 says: "Everyone must submit himself to the governing authorities, for there is no authority except that which God has established. The authorities that exist have been established by God. Consequently, he who rebels against the authority is rebelling against what God has instituted, and those who do so will bring judgment on themselves" (NIV). Frankly, this is not an easy passage to either understand or accept. Our natural minds rebel against this statement that all authority comes from God, since we see so much evidence that many people in authority are neither godly nor competent. Can their authority be God-given? What about the person who has risen to his or her level of incompetency?

The apostle Paul is teaching us that God has established authority as the order for the universe. We see it in every part of creation; some things have authority over others. And if it were not for the principle of authority, we would have nothing but chaos.

The same is true in our business world. We require authority in order to operate a business of any kind. The buck has to stop somewhere. Therefore, the people in positions of authority are part of God's plan for authority. And as Christians, we are directed to submit ourselves to those people who have risen to those authority positions. To rebel against that is to rebel against God's order, and, Paul said, it will bring judgment on us.

Obviously, there have been and are people in positions of authority who should never be there. But that was true when Paul wrote this letter to the Romans. The principle still holds true; we may not respect the people themselves, but we must respect their position.

Well, how do you apply it when you don't feel it? You do it by faith, not by feelings. You pray it into your life on a daily basis. You read those verses from Romans 13 often, and you ask God to change your attitude and your thinking so that you can accept their authority.

First Timothy 2:1–2 tells us to offer requests, prayers, intercession, and thanksgiving for everyone, for kings and all those in authority, that we may live peaceful and quiet lives in all godliness and holiness. We are to pray for those in authority, and we are to pray for peaceful relationships. Now, if you're dealing with an incompetent or impossible boss, have you been praying for him or her regularly? How have you been praying for that person? This is where it starts, and until you begin to truly pray for them, you won't see much change in your attitude or in their behavior.

Maintaining excellent performance. The second thing that I learn from our 1 Peter passage is that I must make sure I am doing my duty, that I am not in any way to blame for the unpleasantness my manager is demonstrating. You see, what Peter goes on to say in this passage is that it is commendable if we bear up under unfair treatment. That kind of suffering finds favor with God. Now I ask you, wouldn't you like to know that God is pleased with you and finds favor with you? That is special recognition. Well, it can be yours if you endure this difficult situation with your boss by doing your duty and being patient.

If part of the problem, however, is that you're not doing your work well, you're not being obedient, or you're not motivated as highly as you should be, then what credit is it, Peter says, if you endure the harsh treatment you are receiving? You're simply enduring what you deserve, and that gets no special recognition.

But if you are indeed doing your duty and you still bear patiently with a difficult and impossible boss, you are doing something truly worthwhile in God's sight.

Sharing the sufferings of Christ. Why is this kind of suffering so precious to God? Peter goes on to tell us it is because that is the way Christ suffered; and when we endure unjust treatment with patience and tolerance, we are sharing in his suffering. That is the example that Christ left us. He did not talk back when he was falsely accused. He didn't threaten anyone, but he kept entrusting himself to God.

Peter says we, too, are called to suffer unjustly! Can you believe that? When this passage was first becoming real to me,

I said, "Lord, that is really tough—*called* to suffer unjustly! I don't want to be treated unfairly."

Don't feel guilty if you have that reaction. None of us in the flesh can want to suffer unjustly. None of us would ask for it or seek after it. But though I didn't want to be treated unfairly, I did want to follow in the steps of Christ and find favor with God. Therefore, I could truthfully say, "Lord, I want to follow you and obey you and please you. Therefore, if it is to your glory for me to continue enduring this impossible boss, I accept it not because I look forward to it, but because I want to please you."

The results of Peter's principle. Let me tell you what starts to happen when you change your thinking and your attitude and apply Peter's principle to your working world. The sting goes out of the situation. Your boss may continue to be impossible, but with an eternal viewpoint and a different motivation, it won't get to you the way it used to. I'm not saying it will be pleasant, but it just will not upset you so much anymore.

I can testify to this. I couldn't believe the changes I saw in myself. As I continued to apply these principles to my situation, I was amazed to realize that this particular impossible boss just could not get to me anymore. I didn't take things personally; I didn't get upset; I didn't think of it once I walked out of the office. The sting was gone, and when the sting goes, it isn't that difficult to endure.

Does the Bible have any practical help when we're faced with an impossible boss? Oh, yes indeed. However, it probably isn't what you'd like to hear. Our human natures would rather have sympathy and pity and condolence and retribution and revenge. But the miracle is that God's principles work and our way doesn't. We are called to die to our natural selves, and death never seems attractive. But when we accept his truth, then we can be alive to him. That death to self that you dread so much is really your avenue to freedom and peace.

My friend, Joan, experienced an unfair situation recently at her job. Someone else was given a promotion that truly should have been hers. And she was upset; who wouldn't be? She wanted to go in and tell her boss off and tell the other girl off and let them know that she knew she had been had. She was angry.

I said to her, "Can you go back in there and love that girl, and treat her especially well? Can you keep your mouth closed and not defend yourself or seek revenge? Can you maintain respect for your boss's authority, even though he has treated you wrongly?"

I pointed out to her that if she behaved that way she would have an undeniable witness in that office. After all, everyone else knew that she had gotten a bad deal, and they all knew how they would react if it happened to them. So they were looking for the same kind of reaction from her. But if, instead, they saw her react with kindness and love and a gentle spirit, they would have to take notice. How could that be explained? They would wonder how she could do that.

Joan went back and did the right thing. She was kind to the girl who got the promotion, and she didn't let her boss have it. The next time I saw her, I asked how it had gone. She reported that she had applied this biblical principle, and somehow the promotion didn't really seem so important to her anymore.

A couple of weeks later she reported that she was actually thankful she didn't get that promotion, because it required lots of overtime and the girl in the job was having quite a lot of trouble. Joan could see that God had protected her from a very difficult position. I asked her, "Who won? You died to yourself and you did what was totally contrary to your human desires. But tell me, who won?" She looked at me, and quietly said, "I did."

Why are we so slow to learn that principle? We are the winners when we go God's way—even to the point of dying to ourselves. He is not a cruel taskmaster. He has told us that his yoke is easy and his burden is light. Our method will not be easy. If we insist on doing things our way and carrying the load all by ourselves, it will not be a light load. It will be heavy and dreary and terribly difficult.

The Incompetent Boss

Smart employees understand that their job description includes making the boss look good. The world uses that principle as a manipulative tool, but we have other reasons to do it. First Corinthians 13 describes the kind of love we are to develop in our lives, a love that is like God's love. And that kind of love "does not delight in evil but rejoices with the truth. It always protects, always trusts, always hopes, always perseveres" (NIV).

As Christians we are to ever be seeking to have God's love fill us and overflow through us to everyone in our lives, including our incompetent bosses. Therefore, we should try to make them look good, not for manipulation purposes, but because God's love motivates us to protect others from bad exposure, to delight in the good things they do, not the bad things, to try to cover up their mistakes whenever we can.

Proverbs 17:9 says, "He who covers over an offense promotes love, but whoever repeats the matter separates close friends" (NIV). One of the typical things that happens when we encounter an incompetent boss is that we talk about that person in derogatory ways. It's easy to do. A friend was sharing with me that her boss is very difficult and no one agrees with the way her boss runs the department. She has no trouble gaining confirmation from her coworkers that her negative attitude toward her boss is justified; everyone feels the same way.

It's likely, if you truly work for an incompetent boss, that everyone else feels the same way you do, and therefore, at lunch and on breaks that's what you talk about. Instead of covering up the offense, you repeat the matter and make the situation much worse. So take a positive approach—stop talking about him or her to other people. Pray for that boss; talk to the Lord; get counsel from respected Christians outside the company. But don't be a part of the office gossip and character assassination that usually happens when you have this type of boss.

Ecclesiastes 10:20 says: "Do not revile the king even in your thoughts, or curse the rich in your bedroom, because a bird of the air may carry your words, and a bird on the wing may report what you say" (NIV). Now, Solomon is giving us some very good advice here. To paraphrase, he says: Don't talk about anybody behind their backs, particularly people in authority and control. Those words seem to always get back to them. Many people have done irreparable damage to their careers with loose tongues. Remember, you don't have to say everything you think!

When these biblical principles are in place in your life, then you can start to consider whether it is ever right to confront an incompetent boss or blow the whistle on them. There aren't any black-and-white answers here because the circumstances would dictate what type of action to take. However, I believe confrontation or exposure should be the last thing we do, after other attempts have failed, and after much prayer.

Here are some guidelines to consider in deciding whether or not to confront incompetent bosses: Is their incompetency affecting the quality of the product or service the customer receives? Is their inability to manage causing unfair treatment for employees, others as well as yourself? Are they doing things contrary to your organization's stated standards and policies? In other words, is there a larger picture here than simply your own irritations and frustrations at having to work for an incompetent manager?

If you're convinced there is a larger picture, then confrontation may be advisable. But, again, this must be done with great respect for their authority. You look for ways to make suggestions for improvement without pointing the finger at them. You try to find a way to make it look like their idea to which you are contributing. You do everything you can not to undermine their own self-image.

Incompetent bosses are likely to be very insecure. They are most probably quite aware of their shortcomings, though they may not be able to openly admit them or talk about them. Indeed, they may deny them. But underneath the facade, you can be fairly certain they are insecure about their performance. Therefore, they're going to be worried about someone else showing them up and exposing their shortcomings.

If we truly want to help our incompetent manager to improve, we have to make our suggestions with carefully chosen words. I am not suggesting we use flattery or deceit of any kind. But if we look long enough, we can find something good to say about them and to them, something positive to lead off with, some way to confront without seeming confrontational.

I know it's not easy, but let me tell you this—it's a whole lot easier than doing it the other way. If you've been stewing and fretting over your incompetent boss, if you're constantly frustrated because you want to get rid of him or her or tell them off, if you've been angry at having to put up with their incompetency when you know you could do it better—tell me, has that been easy?

Of course not. It's a more natural reaction than following biblical principles, but it's not easier on you or anyone else. It's harder, and it takes a much greater mental and emotional toll on you. Doesn't it make sense, then, to simply ask God to give you his perspective and his power to deal with your incompetent boss in a Christlike way? The good news is, because of Jesus we have the power to do it. But we have to be willing to allow him to do it through us.

Accepting an Impossible Boss

Can you thank God for putting that impossible boss in your life in order to lead you into a deeper life of trust in him? With eternity's values in mind, can you agree that it is more important to learn more about God and his love for you and to grow in grace and faith in him than it is to be delivered from an impossible boss?

It is not easy to accept that impossible boss. In no way would I represent that this kind of unjust suffering is a piece of cake. But I do believe that accepting it from God's hands and letting him guide us in our reactions—even to the point of suffering unjustly—is easier than our normal human reactions of anger and bitterness and vengeance.

8

Dealing with Men
on the Job

The Book of Genesis explains to us that it was God's plan to create two sexes, male and female, both created equally in his image, both finding the other attractive, both needing each other, and both different in many ways from the other. It was a good plan and it's still good today, one that has brought a great deal of joy, happiness, and fulfillment into the lives of both women and men.

True, the plan has been misused and abused through the ages, and the relationship between men and women certainly has caused many problems and heartaches. But that results from sin coming into the picture, our lack of understanding of each other, and our unwillingness to allow these relationships to be controlled by God's principles.

Now, with many more women in the workplace, we face the challenge of interacting with each other in this environment. Often we have close working relationships with the opposite sex, spending many hours each day working together, physically near each other, and communicating frequently.

Sometimes, we are not aware of the dynamics of these male/female relationships; many of us are in unfamiliar territory. I remember when I began my career as a sales representative for IBM. I was the only woman in my office—I can still see that large sales office, jammed with desks to accommodate about forty salespeople, and there I was in the middle, surrounded by men on every side.

Sounds like a dream come true for a single woman, you say? Well, while I certainly enjoyed the attention that my unique situation afforded me, I discovered quickly that I was not prepared to deal with the many diverse complications that arose from the male/female aspect of it.

From my own experience, I know how easy it is to make the wrong moves and not deal with these male/female encounters appropriately. Therefore, I think it is important to address this subject directly and candidly, because many of you are still struggling with this very problem.

Male Friendships on the Job

There's no doubt that friendships can and do develop between male and female coworkers. Why not become friends with those whom we respect, enjoy, and share many experiences? I can think of several men I've worked with whom I consider good friends, even years later. Friendships are good things, and I'm always grateful for friends, wherever I find them.

However, we must put up the caution flag and be aware of the pitfalls that we can fall into with any friend of the opposite sex. In my case, I'm a single woman, and my male coworker friends are married. That sends up a flag to me that says it is my responsibility to make certain that their wives are comfortable with my friendship with their husbands, and they understand the nature of our relationships.

As these friendships developed, I became very good friends with their wives and families. They were invited to my home and I to theirs. I was certain that they were not concerned in any way about my working relationship with their husbands.

Had I sensed that it bothered them in any way, I would have backed away from that relationship, even though their concerns would have been totally unfounded.

A young man once asked my opinion about having a business luncheon with a woman alone, and he went on to explain that this seemed to bother his new wife. My advice was that if it bothered her, regardless of how innocent or how convenient that business lunch might be, he should do everything possible to schedule those meetings in the office rather than at lunch. I think he should do everything he can to allay his wife's concern.

Some might say we should never have a business lunch alone with someone of the opposite sex, but I honestly don't see this as a black-and-white situation. The business lunch has become a way of life, and it can be an efficient way to conduct business. In itself there is nothing immoral or questionable about it.

But each situation is different and requires wisdom and insight on our part. I think the rule of thumb should be: If in doubt, don't. Or if it bothers your conscience, don't. We know from Romans 14 that there are some disputable matters where sincere Christians will have differing convictions; the important thing for us is not to condemn others but to be certain we follow what we believe is right for us to do.

A suggestion is to bring a third party along. That's usually possible to do, and that solves the question of how it might look to others. Because while working in corporate America most of my peers were men, I usually went to lunch with men. But rarely was it alone.

Male Subordinates

With more and more women now holding management positions, it is no longer uncommon to find women managers with men reporting to them. This has broken new ground for men and women and frequently presents problems for these women managers in knowing just how to relate to their subordinates.

I've encountered many women who struggle with a basic question in this regard: Should a Christian woman hold a position of leadership over men? The question is an outgrowth of the strong conviction of many evangelical Christians that women should not have leadership roles over men within the church. This position is based on passages in 1 Corinthians 14:34–35 and 1 Timothy 2:9–15. Christian women who have been immersed in the conviction that it is wrong to hold leadership positions over men in the church environment quite naturally question whether that principle extends to all leadership positions, including the business world. It is a legitimate question, and it should be confronted.

At this point, I will not get into the question of leadership roles for women in the church but will limit myself to working environments. As I look at Scripture, I can find no directive to women that would prohibit them from holding management positions, including positions of leadership over men.

To the contrary, I can think of many women within Scripture who were leaders. Deborah was a judge over her nation, and she led an army of men into battle (Judg. 4 and 5). The Proverbs 31 woman had both a manufacturing and a real estate business, which easily could have put her in a position of directing male subordinates. We know she managed her household of many servants, and presumably that would include male servants. Lydia was a seller of purple (Acts 16), which was a most prestigious position. She must have interacted with men and directed them at times. We know she had a large household under her management, and this household would most likely have included men.

With no biblical directive prohibiting women from being leaders on the job, I believe a Christian woman is free to hold management positions with male subordinates, if she desires to do so and has the opportunity. However, this can be difficult at times, as we learn how to deal with the men who report to us. Let me point out a few areas here that could present problems.

Because the territory is new, many of us overreact by trying to be too assertive and working too hard at establishing our authority. We may be a little insecure in these new roles, and it is easy to overcompensate by being too rigid and demanding. On the other hand, some women bend over too far backward to keep from intimidating male subordinates and to avoid coming on too strong, and this can cause us to be weak managers who lack proper control.

In my prayer journal I have a list of vulnerable areas in my life, places I recognize as possible satanic strongholds. One is my tendency to overreact, and I continually ask God to deliver me from that propensity. Make it a matter of prayer that God will show you, too, how to walk that middle line, that you may find your own balance as a manager, and that you may not go to extremes in dealing with male subordinates.

Additionally, when we encounter a male subordinate who resents having a female manager, we have a delicate situation on our hands. This is certainly an appropriate time to ask for special wisdom from God, as he has promised us in James 1:5. Patience and endurance will likely be required of us.

There is no reason to be intimidated by this male subordinate, and we have a responsibility to require adequate performance from him. After all, if you are his manager, you have earned your position and he must learn to respect that. But your best hope of winning his respect and dispelling his negative attitude toward you in most cases is to ignore his attitude as much as possible and manage him as you would any other employee. If you are fair and kind in your dealings with him, as a Christian should always be, while at the same time doing the best job possible in your own position, he will probably change his attitude toward you eventually. It may take more time than you would like, but it can happen.

Try to put yourself in your employee's shoes, and recognize that there could be any number of reasons for his behavior. He may feel threatened by having a woman manager or his background could have prejudiced him against women in business. Whatever his reasons, instead of getting angry at him or being vindictive, ask God to give you compassion and tolerance. This is a wonderful opportunity to demonstrate the difference that Jesus Christ makes in our lives.

Once again, Proverbs 16:21 is most helpful: "Sweetness of speech increases persuasiveness." It really is important for us to watch the way we talk in these sensitive situations and to remember to make our speech palatable. Find ways to make your directions and your ideas easy to handle for these male subordinates. It won't diminish your stature to go out of your way to ease the tension for them. And it will increase your persuasiveness. It is a biblical principle I've proven in my own life time and again.

Sexual Harassment

I want to address a topic that has become extremely visible lately: sexual harassment on the job. Recently someone told me how she and her female coworkers endured many years of sexual harassment from the top man in their organization. He continually made sexual remarks to them, asked them for sexual favors, threatened their jobs or promotions or raises if they did not cooperate or if they reported him. He was such a Dr. Jekyll and Mr. Hyde that others found it difficult to believe he could be that way. He chose carefully the women he harassed, making sure he had plenty of leverage and power over them, while at the same time never harassing others so that they would always deny the allegations against him. Only recently were they able to take any action, when their organization formed a committee for grievances. These women, after years of enduring his harassment, sought some legal advice and threatened a class action against the company. As a result, he was quietly urged to resign, which he did.

She shared with me the pain and stress of those years and the turmoil she went through in deciding whether to be a part of the action against him. She wondered if that was the thing a Christian should do; it went against her nature to take such legal action against another person. But I assured her she had done exactly the right thing.

I truly believe that it is not only our right but our responsibility to expose real sexual harassment so that other women can be spared the horror. Otherwise, by doing nothing, we allow it to perpetuate. When we confront and accuse for the good of others as well as ourselves, we are usually on good scriptural ground. Jesus certainly took strong action and had strong words of condemnation for those who were doing wrong and victimizing others in his day.

I know this is not easy for women to do, because you can risk your career and your reputation. You need counsel and great wisdom. But you also need courage to do the right thing.

Now, I also have some compassion for men who feel the climate is so sensitive that anything they say or do could be misinterpreted by a woman who is looking for an excuse to attack. These pendulums do swing in violent directions; balance is a rare commodity. But you know, if our conversations are circumspect, if we say and do only things that we would say and do if Jesus were right there with us, we won't have to worry about false accusations. I would say to the men who have that concern to just treat the women you work with the way Jesus would treat them, and you can put your mind at rest.

Jesus many times made it a point to break traditional laws concerning how women should be treated in his day. By his actions we can be assured that he did not approve of prejudicial attitudes toward women. He talked to women in public, he allowed them to be a part of his traveling entourage and to support his ministry, and he showed them great respect, all of which broke the Jewish traditions.

I am certain he would never approve of some of the prejudicial attitudes I have seen among men today, even some Christian men. I think all of us need to pray a lot about the attitudes we harbor in our hearts.

The Possibility of an Attraction

In a male/female business relationship, because of our natural tendency to be attracted to the opposite sex, and because of the amount of time spent together on a daily basis, an attraction may very well occur. Most of us have seen this happen or have experienced it ourselves. What does a Christian working woman do when she feels an attraction to a male coworker?

The first moment you have any inkling that you may be developing an attraction for a man on your job or he for you, ask yourself one critical question: Are either of you married?

When One or Both of You Are Married

If the answer to that question is yes, your course of action is clear. The principle set forth in the Bible is unequivocal: People who are married can allow no intimate relationships with people of the opposite sex. You must not allow any words or feelings or looks or innuendos to be exchanged between you and this man. That is it! Final! If it means changing jobs or asking to be transferred, do it. There is no middle ground.

You may think it unnecessary to emphasize such an obvious truth, but as Christian women in a society that gives little respect or regard to marriage vows, we need to remind ourselves of these basic Christian principles. Have you noticed how easy it is for us to lower our standards to those of the world around us instead of motivating others to raise their standards to those of God's Word?

It would be nice if these attractions only happened to single, available people, but that is not the case. I have happily married friends in the working world who still must be on their guard against an attraction developing with men in their work environment.

Let me hasten to add that these attractions are not limited to working women. They are possible whether or not a woman leaves her home every morning to go to work. However, it is fair to say that most working women meet and interact with more men than women who do not work, and therefore the opportunities for developing these attractions are more prevalent. This simply means that as Christian working women, we must be aware of the dangers that could await us.

The answer is the same even if one of the people involved is experiencing a difficult marriage. Many times couples tend to justify illegitimate relationships by rationalizing that one of them is in an unhappy marriage. The condition of the marriage in no way changes the principle by which we should abide. As Christians, we should do everything possible to help hurting marriages find healing. Allowing a relationship to develop with a person whose marriage is shaky will do just the opposite.

In today's society such a position appears to be drastic, legalistic, eccentric, and inflexible. But that's because we have become so infiltrated with the world's philosophy that basic Christian principles now appear unrealistic. Remember, God's principles work. While they are ageless, they are not outdated, they are not old-fashioned. That is simply Satan's lie, which many people have bought.

Satan is a master liar, and he wants us to think that we cannot be happy or contented living under God's principles. But he cannot make good on his promises. All of us could tell of people we know, or perhaps of our own experience, where lives have been harmed by disobeying this Christian principle. Satan makes people believe that he can give them more happiness and fulfillment if they will do it his way, but just the opposite is true.

The only acceptable course of action for a Christian is to discontinue the relationship and avoid any further possibility of allowing that attraction to increase. And the break must be drastic and definite. If you think you can have long talks, quiet lunches, or innocent encounters in such a relationship without ever allowing it out of bounds, you don't understand chemistry too well or you have too much confidence in yourself.

Don't be fooled by rationalizing that you are just being a good friend. You will be opening yourself to immense temptation, and chances are you will succumb. Many times illegitimate relationships begin because one of those involved is a good listener. How many times have I heard a woman say, "He didn't have anyone else he could talk with. I was the only friend he had, and I just couldn't be cold and unkind to him."

If he needs help and counseling, you are the wrong person to give it. Certainly it is possible for him to find help in other places and people. There is no good reason for you to ever allow a wrong relationship to develop. It isn't only a question of that chemistry getting out of hand. A nonsexual relationship that becomes emotionally intimate to the point that it takes something away from the marriage is a form of unfaithfulness.

Many times we women are allured by male attention, and as we begin to enjoy the nice feeling of having a male presence in our life, we want to forget that it is an improper relationship. That is a very easy trap for us to fall into.

No matter how flattering it may be to you to have that male attention, though, forget it. Drop it, and drop it fast. The sooner you do, the better. Take whatever steps are necessary to insure that you are not tempted to let that relationship develop beyond the professional and business level. To do anything else is to give Satan a foothold in your life.

Ephesians 4:27 warns us that we should not give the devil any such opportunity. Proverbs 4:26–27 says, "Watch the path of your feet, and all your ways will be established. Do not turn to the right nor to the left; turn your foot from evil." The correct course of action is clear for Christians. It is our responsibility to keep our feet riveted to the right path, not turning for an instant to the right or to the left. Jesus said:

> If your hand or your foot causes you to stumble, cut it off and throw it from you; it is better for you to enter life crippled or lame, than having two hands or two feet, to be cast into the eternal fire. And if your eye causes you to stumble, pluck it out, and throw it from you. It is better for you to enter life with one eye, than having two eyes, to be cast into the fiery hell.
>
> Matthew 18:8–9

When Both of You Are Single

If you are single and so is he, then what do you do when you're attracted to a man with whom you work? Assuming that he is a Christian (because you would not ever want to be seriously interested in a man who was not), you need to carefully think through the effect of having a relationship with a coworker.

There is no scriptural guideline on this one, but common sense tells us that such a relationship can cause complications. It tends to distract you from your job, and other coworkers may resent it if they feel it is affecting your work or their workload. It is almost impossible to keep these relationships quiet; usually everyone is aware. You may think no one knows, but that is rarely the case.

Certainly, if one of you is in management and the other is not, you will be exposing yourself to widespread criticism. That kind of situation can easily lead to conflict of interest; or conversely, you may bend over so far backward to avoid conflict of interest that your own career could suffer as a result.

If it appears that this relationship may become established and regular, it might be a good idea for one of you to try to change jobs or departments. You'll be able to work in a more relaxed fashion, do a better job, and enjoy your relationship with more freedom.

However, I do know of an instance where two single people were able to keep a relationship totally separate from their work environment, and they worked together as peers for two or three years without a problem. They were both mature people who never talked about the relationship at work, rarely had lunch together, or socialized on the job whatsoever. When their careers eventually led them to different departments though, it was much more comfortable for both of them.

Try to be objective if you find yourself in such circumstances. Find someone who knows the situation and can be trusted, and ask for counsel. This is a case where other respected opinions would be greatly useful to you.

In summary, if we approach this male/female part of our business lives with a commitment to uphold the name of Jesus Christ and to make certain that nothing in our lives brings dishonor to him, we will have the appropriate attitude and he will give us guidance as we work our way through what can often be "touchy" situations. We are living in enemy territory, so to speak, for we are not of this world, though we are in it, as Jesus told us in John 17:15–16. Therefore, in a sense we are in a fishbowl in our working worlds, on view for all to see if our claim of Christianity makes any real difference in our lives.

It is a wonderful opportunity to show a watching world that

Christ is a reality. But we must live extremely circumspect lives, avoiding any appearance of evil. A passage from 1 Peter 2:12 and 15 (NIV) gives us a clear directive in this respect:

> Live such good lives among the pagans that, though they accuse you of doing wrong, they may see your good deeds and glorify God on the day he visits us. . . . For it is God's will that by doing good you should silence the ignorant talk of foolish men.

With the world watching us once we declare ourselves followers of the Lord, our lives must be lived in such a manner that they cannot, though they try, accuse us truthfully of wrongful lives.

I believe that particularly in this area of relating to men on the job we must be especially certain that our behavior is circumspect. Go the extra mile where necessary. Leave no room for doubt. Remember, we carry the reputation of Jesus Christ with us; we are his representatives. It is a marvelous, and at the same time grave, responsibility. We must not take it lightly.

9

Profanity,
Off-Color Jokes,
and Sexual Propositions

Some of us try to act as though we didn't hear it; some of us grin our way through, hoping no one will notice how uncomfortable we are; some of us blast out in loud protest, embarrassing and alienating people in the process. Profanity and suggestive conversation are difficult to avoid in the working world, and often we just don't know how to deal with it.

As I think back over my work experience, I realize that I've reacted in all of those ways at one time or another. When I was just starting in my sales career, I tried very hard to be accepted by everyone, so I never objected to any language used in my presence for fear of alienating someone. In fact, sadly, I was a participant at times during those years when I was running from God. At other times I've shifted in my chair uncomfortably, not knowing how to react to a dirty joke (and sometimes I still do!). Occasionally I've objected in a manner that was judgmental and made others unnecessarily uncomfortable, which was not an effective way to deal with the problem either.

The Acceptance of Profanity

Not too many of us can escape a working environment where profanity and other inappropriate language are present. Our society has made it acceptable for bad language to be used in almost any setting. Over the years I've noticed that more and more people are using profanity. It's commonplace, and it's not limited to less-educated people. In fact, some seem to think it makes them more sophisticated and trendy.

It's almost laughable when you think about it, because the use of profanity really indicates a lack of individuality, a lack of self-control, a lack of good taste, and a limited vocabulary— traits that are not attractive in successful businesspeople. Yet when it comes to the language that is used, these common, low, demeaning, vulgar, trite words and expressions have come to be accepted and expected in most working environments.

Because profanity is so accepted, I think many Christians are intimidated by it or have become so accustomed to it that they rarely express any opposition to it. In fact, sad to say, I fear many Christians hear it so much that they lose sight of its evil and eventually participate themselves.

Biblical Principles

What are some principles or guidelines to help us in dealing with the people around us who continually use profanity and tell off-color jokes—whose general conversation is suggestive and inappropriate? And how do we as women deal with sexual propositions or suggestions?

The first thing is to make absolutely certain that we are in no way participants. Without any doubt, this kind of talk is totally off-limits for a Christian who desires to be truly committed to Jesus Christ. Let's look at two of the many appropriate passages that deal with our language.

In all things show yourself to be an example of good deeds, with purity in doctrine, dignified, sound in speech which is beyond reproach, in order that the opponent may be put to shame, having nothing bad to say about us.

Titus 2:7–8

Let no one look down on your youthfulness, but rather in speech, conduct, love, faith and purity, show yourself an example of those who believe.

1 Timothy 4:12

Our speech should be a distinguishing mark of our Christianity. In an environment where profanity is the norm, we, as Christians, should stand out as lights in the darkness. It should quickly be obvious to everyone that we never engage in any kind of talk or conversation or joke that even comes close to being off-color or impure. No one we work with should ever be able to remember hearing a profane word come out of our mouths.

This is a cut-and-dried, black-and-white area, clearly set forth in Scripture, and we must obey without any thought as to the consequences. We shouldn't even stop to worry about how we will be perceived if our language is different from everyone else's because we never use profane or inappropriate language. Regardless of whether they think of us as religious fanatics, our course is still clear: In no way should any questionable language proceed from our mouths.

That is the first guideline in dealing with profanity. In many cases, as your peers become aware that you never participate in the slightest bit of off-color language or jokes, it will dry up when you're around. If you notice that people change the subject when you walk in or apologize for bad language in your presence, I think it should be considered as a compliment. Your testimony should be that clear.

Most people will admire and respect you for this commitment to pure speech, even if they never tell you that or even if they tease you about it. Few people are committed to any principles, and when they see it in you, they will notice. Don't forget that you're being watched, often by the one or ones you would least expect to be watching you; and when they see a consistent purity of language from you, they will take note.

Appropriate Responses to Profanity

Many times, however, people do not care at all if you're offended and may even step up their level of profanity just because they know it bothers you. What are some other steps you can take to combat this kind of environment?

Stan had worked many years for his firm. He had a lot of seniority and a good job. Suddenly, the company was sold, and there was a complete change in top management. Stan was asked to stay, but before too long he had a good offer from another company. It was a hard decision for him to make. His old job was near home, he had lots of friends at work, and there were all those years invested in the company. One day Stan came out of a meeting, very much like many of his coworkers under the new management, with his mind made up—to leave. The language used at the meetings was coarse beyond belief. Stan just wasn't comfortable there anymore.

If you're in a particularly offensive environment, getting out of it may be your best course of action, as it was for Stan. No job is worth subjecting yourself to continual coarse language.

Aside from changing jobs, there are other ways to deal with profanity, inappropriate conversations, and dirty jokes. First, anything you say or do must come from a heart of love and compassion, not from a "holier than thou" attitude. It cannot come in a condemning way, and should not put the offender on the spot or make them look bad, if at all possible. Pray for these people and ask God to give you his love and compassion for them.

Here are some suggestions: When others use the name of our precious Lord as profanity, which is the worst kind of profanity, stop them quietly and gently ask if they know him. They will usually look at you and say, "What?" And you simply say, "Well, you use his name an awful lot, and I just wondered if you really know him—Jesus Christ? I know him; he's my Savior, my friend, my Lord." Something along that line will either stop them cold and cause them to change the subject, or it could open up an opportunity to explain to them who Jesus really is. But it must be done gently, without a condemning attitude.

Another possibility is to say, "You know, if you used my mother's name as a curse word, I wouldn't hesitate to stop and object very strongly. But I'm sure you would have too much respect to use my mother's name in a degrading way. Yet Jesus Christ is far more precious to me than even my mother, and it really is painful to me to hear you use his name as a curse word."

Lou, a lawyer, handles this kind of profanity by asking if the person realizes what the Bible says about the end result of using God's name in vain. He reminds them of the second commandment, which says that anyone who takes God's name in vain will not go unpunished. He approaches it as though doing them a favor, to alert them to the consequences of their actions, rather than because he is offended at their language. That's a strong approach, but if you knew Lou, you could well imagine how effectively he could carry it off.

Occasionally, I have said something like, "Why do you use his name? There are many other people in history whose names you could use. Why not George Washington, King Henry IV, Mohammed, or Buddha? Why do you only use Jesus Christ as a curse word?" That really makes people stop and think. They will usually reply that it's just a bad habit. But now the door is open for you to explain that the name of Jesus is a name more highly honored by God than any other name. And we know from Scripture that someday at his name every knee shall bow and every tongue confess that he is Lord (see Phil. 2:9–10).

It is for this reason, of course, that through the ages our enemy, Satan, has done everything possible to damage and harm the name of Jesus Christ. He knows that power and forgiveness and new life are in that name, and he wants to destroy it. He hates the name of Jesus.

If you explain why Jesus' name is used rather than any other historical or religious person, it gives you a wonderful opportunity to talk about our Savior. It could be an effective opening for a witness.

Dealing with Vulgar Language and Jokes

Words and jokes that are just distasteful and vulgar, though offensive, do not, in my opinion, demand the same bold stand that the use of our Lord's name does, and I rarely say anything against it. I simply avoid it as much as possible. Sometimes it may be appropriate to use body language and facial expressions to show that we consider such remarks inappropriate.

When I'm caught in a group from which I cannot escape—such as a meeting—and an off-color joke is told, I usually just endure it. But I in no way show any approval or acceptance of the joke. We are not required to appreciate these kinds of jokes or remarks, even when they come from upper management. In situations where it's possible for me to leave, I try to leave as quietly as possible and simply remove myself from the environment.

If you're encountering peers or coworkers who insist on telling dirty jokes in your presence and it's not possible to escape, you may find it appropriate to address them directly about it, and simply request that they wait until you're out of earshot to repeat their jokes. It is difficult to do this without coming off as "Suzy Spiritual," and we don't want to be offensive if we can avoid it.

Jesus' Instructions and Example

I'm reminded that our Lord didn't worry about offending people in cases where he felt the issue was important enough. Many times he stated his opposition to things and people, and his words were strong and undeniably offensive. His purpose was not to offend people, but rather to defend what he knew demanded his defense. Our Lord's beautiful balance models how we should act and react in offensive circumstances. Certain times will call for righteous anger and indignation, while other times a quiet and gentle reaction is the best course.

It all requires prayer and sensitivity on our part. If you're in the midst of these kinds of circumstances, give it a great deal of prayer time—and be sure you remain compassionate and kind.

If you are belligerent toward the people involved, you probably need to work on your attitude first. It's very important that we don't assume the appearance of condemnation. We don't want to project the attitude that Christianity is totally negative or that Christians are just against everything. It is a fine line to walk, and it requires much prayer.

The issue is not that our Christian ears cannot tolerate this language or that we are contaminated by it. Jesus said that though we are in this world, we are not of it. He further prayed to his Father, not that we should be removed from this world, but that we should be kept from the evil one (John 17:14–16). It is not his aim to shield us from every worldly environment. Rather, he has purposed to leave us here in the midst of this worldly environment as witnesses.

And that means we will be subjected to hearing and seeing things contrary to our beliefs and God's standards. But we can learn a wonderful trick of tuning out and focusing our minds on good things when surrounded by bad language. And sometimes that is more appropriate than a verbal response.

I just wonder if, when the Lord was eating with the notorious sinners of his day, he heard language that was inappropriate? That wouldn't be surprising, and I would imagine that if he did, he handled it tactfully and gently. I could imagine at some times he might not even rebuke people for those vulgar words and phrases, which were a part of their everyday conversation. He knew that their hearts had to be changed first, and his presence would soon send a message that this Man was not ordinary, and ordinary language was not acceptable.

The Familiar Double Standard

Quite often I have had colleagues apologize to me for the use of bad language in my presence, whether from them or someone else. They seemed to feel that bad language was reserved for men only.

In a sense I appreciate that they identify me as a lady who doesn't approve of bad language. But on more than one occasion I have said, "If the language is inappropriate for my ears, it is just as inappropriate for male ears."

Women don't have particularly sensitive ears that cannot accept what men's ears can. This is a double standard that just doesn't make sense. Good taste and appropriate language are the same for male and female, so this eliminates the need for two sets of vocabularies—one when women are present and one when they're not. I find that kind of double standard very hypocritical and indefensible.

Sexual Advances

Sexual remarks and suggestions are another problem we may have to deal with on the job. Let me say categorically that the response to these situations should be the same, no matter where they're encountered, and that is an unqualified, unhesitating "NO!" If you ever stop to consider whether it might harm your career to take a firm stand, you've opened the door for trouble.

How many women have you and I known who've gotten themselves involved with men they work with because of a hesitation on their part to turn a man off for fear it would damage their career? And Christian women are not immune to these temptations. Proverbs 4 gives us strong admonitions about dealing with evil suggestions:

> Do not enter the path of the wicked,
> And do not proceed in the way of evil men.
> Avoid it, do not pass by it;
> Turn away from it and pass on.
>
> verses 14–15

> Let your eyes look directly ahead,
> And let your gaze be fixed straight in front of you.
> Watch the path of your feet,
> And all your ways will be established.
> Do not turn to the right nor to the left;
> Turn your foot from evil.
>
> verses 25–27

I think the writer here is trying to tell us that if we give an evil idea the smallest opportunity, we're really asking for trouble. There's one proper response to sexual suggestions or overtures for a Christian woman, and it is an unqualified "No way!"

Don't for one minute be flattered by these suggestions or advances. That's something to which we women are highly vulnerable—an illicit suggestion, coated in the right words, can sound rather attractive. Remember Proverbs 4, and don't give it one second's thought. If you have to make a mistake in a situation like this, make sure it's on the side of overreacting! Make certain your message is clear: The answer is no now, and it will always be no.

Can we, as Christians in the working world, take a firm yet loving stand against vulgar and inappropriate language, profanity, off-color jokes? I trust you agree with me that the answer is definitely yes. However, without question, it requires much careful thought and sensitivity on our part.

If you find yourself faced with these problems, pray much about them. Then try some of the above suggestions for dealing with them. Remember, we are called to be salt and light in a dark and tasteless world, and the difference in our lives should be visible. A difference that makes others want what we have, rather than turning them off.

10
Handling Pressure and Fatigue

You have probably seen a plaque, paperweight, or bumper sticker with the message: "Women have to work twice as hard and be twice as good as men in order to get ahead. Fortunately, for us it isn't difficult." When I first saw that, I chuckled and said, "That's true." Well, as appealing as that may be to us, it isn't true, because it *is* difficult. We working women often have double duties and responsibilities that pull us in opposite directions. To claim that it isn't difficult is deceptive.

Women who work outside the home are prone to finding themselves in the predicament of being overworked, overcommitted, tired, and exhausted. A lot is expected of us. Many of us not only hold down demanding jobs but run a household as well. We have husbands and children and housework and all that they demand. Some of us are single mothers and do all that work without anyone at home to help share the responsibility. And many of us have responsibility for aging parents and family members besides our home and various outside activities.

On top of that, we have the added pressure these days of proving that we can handle jobs previously held by men only—and we must never let anyone think we're less than totally capable. So, whether real or imagined, we often operate under the impression that we must be superwomen!

How Jesus Handled Fatigue

One thing I've always noticed when reading about the Lord Jesus is that he never seemed to be in a hurry or frustrated, yet obviously he had to be tired and pressured at times. I was reading of the time when he was told that John the Baptist had been beheaded, and he tried to get away for a few days of rest and mourning. But he could not get away from the crowd, even at that painful time. The crowds always pursued him, and he would give up his rest time to minister to their needs.

I read those passages and say to myself, "I want to be that way too. I want to be able to give to others and not worry about my own personal needs. I want to be able to function under pressure and fatigue with the same selflessness that Jesus had. What keeps me from being able to do that?"

I began to analyze the kind of pressure I face and the kind of pressure the Lord faced. My problem, I realized, was not that I had too much to do or that I was overcommitted. It's not possible to be overcommitted to Jesus Christ—and he was overcommitted to the ministry given him if by that you mean that every ounce of his life and energy was given to his ministry. Jesus, however, kept a single focus in his life. Though he touched many people, gave of himself continually, and had many demands on him, he knew exactly what the goal was, what was important and what was not. He didn't try to be everything to everyone.

All Things to All People

What a relief it has been to realize that Jesus sometimes disappointed people. He did not always do what others thought he should do. In Mark 1:35–38, we read of one of these times, after Jesus had been up very late the night before healing people at Capernaum.

And in the early morning, while it was still dark, He arose and went out and departed to a lonely place, and was praying there. And Simon and his companions hunted for Him; and they found Him, and said to Him, "Everyone is looking for You." And He said to them, "Let us go somewhere else to the towns nearby, in order that I may preach there also; for that is what I came out for."

The disciples were urging Jesus to go back into Capernaum, where the crowds were waiting for him. But Jesus, knowing exactly what his purpose was, chose to disappoint that crowd in order to do what he knew was more important.

That is a vital lesson for us to learn. It is not possible to be all things to all people. We must know what takes priority and be willing to let other things go—even if it means disappointing someone.

Reducing the Number of Activities

One of my goals is to get the number of activities in my life reduced to a manageable level. I think many times my problem is not that I put in too many hours, but that my mind and thoughts are divided into so many different areas and activities so that I lack focus. And that's where the frustration sets in.

How can we eliminate activities? I can hear some of you saying, "What can I leave off? There's nothing that's optional!" Well, you might be surprised. The first thing to do is to sit down and make a list of everything that is on your plate to be done right now. Write every responsibility, every job, every involvement—just so you can see in front of your eyes the number and variety of activities you are trying to accomplish. Do the same thing with your duties on your job.

Now, with the list in your hand, ask the Lord to give you wisdom about priorities. Then go down that list one by one and ask yourself the following questions about every item on the list.

• *What would happen if I crossed this job off my list?* You know what I discovered? Many of the things I thought had to be done, didn't! I could cross some items off that list and the world would not come to an end, my friends and family would not desert me, my boss would not fire me, and I would not be thrown in jail. It gave me some perspective.

You will be amazed as you go through your list that much of the pressure you feel is self-imposed. Even on your job, many of your deadlines are not set by your manager but by you. Certainly, nothing is wrong with striving for excellence and being ambitious. But if you are pushing yourself so hard that you're fatigued and frustrated, you won't impress anyone very much. You'll start making mistakes and be difficult to get along with before you know it.

• *What can be postponed to a later time?* Many things that you think have to be done today can easily be done later with no harm done. I remember when I planned to wallpaper my daughter's room. We had chosen the paper, and I wanted to get started right away. But our schedule was truly hectic at that point. And I was getting all uptight about not getting her bedroom finished. She said to me, "Mom, I'm not putting any pressure on you to do that now. It can wait." She was a lot smarter than her mom that time. The pressure was self-imposed, and the job was easily postponed with no harm done.

Understand, I'm not advocating procrastination. Many of us get ourselves into dilemmas by always putting things off. That may be part of the reason you're in that mess you're in now. When something has to be done, the best policy is do it now and do it right. That will save you more time and more headaches than anything else.

But if you've been putting yourself under pressure to get something done, and in reality there is no reason it has to be done immediately, postpone it.

• *Who else could do this besides me?* One of my biggest problems is that I try to do things that others could and would do, if I would just ask. I'm beginning to realize that I am very reluctant to ask people to do things for me. For some reason I feel guilty asking them to do something that I know I can do—especially if it appears that I'm trying to get rid of the dirty work. So, I keep heaping the details on myself to avoid feeling guilty, and then I'm exhausted, and I start to resent having to do everything myself. It gets to be a ridiculous cycle. And it's no one's fault but mine, simply because I haven't asked for any help.

Have you ever noticed that Jesus allowed his disciples to do a lot of the work? They took care of preparations and meals, and they went out two by two healing and casting out demons and telling others about Jesus. They were laborers together with him, and he didn't attempt to meet every demand personally. He shared his ministry with his disciples. We must learn to share with others where we can.

Mothers, do you delegate appropriate responsibilities to your children? Or do you still try to take care of too many of the details, things they really could do for themselves? Maybe guilt feelings drive you to that, because you don't want them to suffer just because they have a working mom. Guilt is one of Satan's best tricks. Your kids are capable of doing a lot more than you think. Shed the guilt, and delegate some of those household chores. Your children will benefit from learning to be responsible, and they'll benefit from having a mom who isn't always tired.

I want you to know, as I keep telling myself, that nobody gives prizes for superwomen! Learn how to ask others to help you. Learn how to admit that you can't do everything all by yourself.

• *What priority does each item remaining on the list deserve?* Stand back with objectivity and really assess which items are truly more important than others, and arrange your list in order of priority. Then plan a schedule—a reasonable schedule with realistic time frames—and start chipping away at the list, one by one. Don't think about the next item while you're trying to work on the first one. Keep your mind clear, focus on the task at hand. And do it now and do it right.

The First Priority

When I get under pressure and time is short, one of the first things I sacrifice is my personal time with the Lord. "After all," I rationalize, "the Lord understands my schedule." For me, it is a constant battle to keep my time with God as my first priority. Unlike our jobs or other demands, there is no time clock to punch with the Lord. He does not issue us strict instructions on when and how long we should be with him daily. He wants our heart's devotion, not a routine we go through to make ourselves feel better.

Since our time with him is just between us and God and we are accountable to no one else, we can begin to use that time as our buffer. If anything has to give, our quiet time with the Lord gives.

No wonder every Christian has to fight continually to keep a consistent, daily time with God. After all, our enemy knows how effective we could be if we spent significant time in prayer and meditation on God's Word every day. And Satan is a fantastic liar. Jesus told us he is a liar and the father of lies, and there is no truth in him (John 8:44). If you are sincerely attempting to establish a consistent walk with God and a life of devotion, don't be surprised to find Satan very actively trying to defeat you. Here are some of the lies he tells us:

- "You don't have any other option. If you take time for prayer today, you won't be able to get to work early, and that report will not be ready in time. It's not your fault. You have to do your work."
- "You worked late last night. In fact, you've been working late a lot this week. You deserve and need a little extra sleep. God will understand."
- "God doesn't expect you to pray and read the Bible every day. After all, you are a working mother with two small children. You never have any time to yourself. You can only do so much. After the children get older, you'll be able to have a devotional life."

- "You're just not a morning person. That's okay. It doesn't matter when you pray. Do it tonight when you get home."
- "Hey, you don't have to do this every day. After all, you are not under the Law anymore. Just do it when you feel like it. God doesn't want you to pray if you don't feel like it."

Undoubtedly, all of us could add to this list. The fact that Satan works so hard to obstruct our time with God should give us some idea of just how important it is.

As I read about Jesus, I see that the more pressure he was under and the more demands that were placed on him, the more he got away and spent time alone in prayer. If Jesus needed that quantity and quality of time in prayer, how much more do we!

It is not a legal requirement, that is true. But after years of working at this, I can tell you it requires discipline. I think we need to be creative and flexible in our devotional life, and for each of us it will be an individual and personal thing. But we must also be disciplined. That means getting up early when you don't want to. That means making yourself read the Bible even when your feelings are numb. It means putting this good habit in place and sticking to it consistently. But oh, what a difference it makes in our lives.

This is the only principle for overcoming fatigue and exhaustion that will work every time: *As the pressures, exhaustion, and fatigue increase, increase your quiet time with God in direct proportion.* Are you absolutely at the end of your rope? Then determine that you will spend a greatly increased amount of time with God. Ignore your feelings. If you're exhausted, you won't feel like doing anything except collapsing. Don't be surprised that you don't feel like spending time with God. Remember this: *Feelings have zero I.Q.* They are not intelligent. Sometimes they're right, sometimes they're wrong. But you can never trust them to be accurate barometers of your spiritual temperature.

Also, don't be afraid to give up sleep time for prayer time. It's no great sacrifice—it's a great privilege. I finally realized that when I took away from prayer time to sleep, the sleep I got did me no good. You won't suffer from spending time with the Lord. Those quiet morning hours, before the world starts to stir, alone with Jesus, will give you perspective and peace and strength to face all the duties you have ahead of you for that day.

Nothing compares with developing a personal, one-on-one relationship with Jesus Christ. As I am writing this, I think of my experience this very morning. As soon as I got up, a worry started to take hold of my mind. I began to think of what I should do to solve this particular problem. Fear started to gnaw at my stomach. My head hurt. In a matter of minutes, I was emotionally "fit to be tied," as we say down South. I did not want to sit still long enough to pray or meditate. I wanted to do something about this particular problem. But by sheer force of will, against all my feelings, I pushed myself into the sofa where I spend time with God. (I find that it helps to have a special spot that is your meeting place with the Lord.) I remembered that I have to bring every thought into captivity (see 2 Cor. 10:5), and I began, slowly, to force my thoughts away from my concern and toward God.

Gradually, the problem came into perspective. Through meditating on who God is, through singing some hymns that reminded me of his faithfulness and protection, through expressing my concern to him, through reading the Bible, through reciting some of his great and precious promises, my fears subsided, my concern was given over to his keeping, and my day then could begin with a light, free spirit. As a matter of fact, God showed me what a great blessing this particular situation could be in my life, because it offers me an opportunity to really trust him in an area that is new to me.

After time spent with God, my entire outlook had changed dramatically. Yes, it took discipline. No, I didn't feel like doing it. But I ask you, who benefited? Instead of facing my day with frustration, with a frantic outlook and with fear, I gained peace and assurance.

If a consistent time with God can give me that kind of outlook, can alleviate my fears, can calm my unrest, and give me direction, am I not then foolish to let anything interfere with it? If time with God is the beginning of finding an answer to my pressures and fatigue, is it not a very poor economy on my part to eliminate that time in my schedule?

I am not a special case. It is no easier for me than for anyone else. I do not always succeed in applying this principle as I should. But I can testify that when I do apply it, it really works. So remember the principle: *As the pressures, exhaustion, and fatigue increase, increase your prayer time in direct proportion.* I believe it is the essential foundational principle for a Christian who is battling pressure and fatigue.

11

The Working Mother

You can usually spot working mothers. They have symptoms that are dead giveaways. They're frequently clock-watchers, waiting until a certain hour when they can call home to make sure that everyone is home when they should be, leaving as soon as they possibly can to get home to their children and the other full-time job that awaits them when they get there. They rarely get to work early, because they are already up at the break of dawn just to get the kids ready and off on time.

Working mothers develop unique skills at telephone negotiation, as they settle arguments, dispense discipline, and issue instructions electronically. They frequently have worried looks, especially when they've left their child with a fever or an upset stomach or when their four-year-old is not happy in the new day-care center.

Talk about fatigue and pressure! They are common symptoms among working mothers, who cook, wash, clean, chauffeur, tutor, and nourish one or more children between 5:00 and 11:00 in the evening, after working hard all day.

When their children are between infancy and about ten years of age, working mothers are usually more physically exhausted than anything else. Those are the years that the children demand a great deal of help with anything they do, from tying their shoes to homework assignments. Those are the years when children frequently do not sleep all night and seem to get sick more often. Once the children reach the teen years, the emotional strain becomes exhausting, as mothers try to cope with the ups and downs of normal teenagers and preteens while holding down a demanding job.

If it's so tough, then, why are so many mothers working? In November 1984, the *New York Times* reported that 60 percent of all mothers work, including 46 percent of those with children younger than three and 52 percent of those with children younger than six (*New York Times,* November 25, 1984). That means that millions of women leave home every day—dropping children at school, day-care centers, or neighbors or relatives' homes—and enter the working world. Why do they do it?

Some work because they really believe, or have bought this generation's philosophy, that a mother who stays home and does nothing but raise her children has little or no ambition or self-esteem and is probably lazy. They believe they'll find the fulfillment that has evaded them as mothers in a job or career. Some work because they've allowed their standard of living to rise to such a level that luxuries now seem like necessities. They feel compelled to keep the family income at a high enough level so that they can have all the material things they've come to regard as necessary. Others work because they truly love their jobs, and they love being moms as well, and they seem to be capable for the most part of balancing the two roles. But many—probably most—of these mothers have no choice; they are contributing support to the family that is necessary to make ends meet. Frequently, they are the sole support of their families. If they didn't work, they would truly be without the basics of life—food, shelter, and clothing.

The Working Mother Guilt Syndrome

I have some firsthand knowledge of what working moms go through because I've been a career mom since my daughter, now grown and married, was eight years old. As I think back over the years, the one emotion that comes flooding back is guilt—guilt because I was not home in the afternoon when Julie got home from school. Guilt because Julie didn't like the sitter much or because I could not go to her school during the day to be a grade mother or take part in cookie sales. Guilt because the time I did have with her was occupied with housework or work brought home from the office. Guilt when she became a latchkey kid in high school years, worrying about her feelings of loneliness. Guilt because she had to do more chores than most of her peers. The list could go on and on.

My whole upbringing and the role model I had in my very special and very traditional mother taught me, subconsciously, that mothers should live their lives for their children, should always be there for their children, should meet their every possible need, and anything less was second best. I honestly cannot remember coming home from school when my mother was not right there, taking care of me and my brothers—cleaning, ironing, cooking, praying—and never wishing she was anything or anyone else.

So guilt was inevitable as I struggled to be a good mom by the standards that I thought represented the best in mothering and at the same time tried to keep up with a growing and demanding career. Obviously, it was not possible for me to be the kind of mom that I thought I should be, so I had to live with the belief that my daughter would have a second-rate mom. There seemed no alternative.

Undoubtedly, many working mothers reading this are experiencing this guilt I've described. And guilt that is not dealt with is a most debilitating, demoralizing emotion to live with. So if you find yourself a guilt-ridden working mother, here are some suggestions on dealing with those feelings.

First, analyze the guilt that you feel. Describe it, at least to yourself, in detail. Write it down if you need to. But be certain that you know specifically what you feel guilty about. Do not allow that guilt to remain just a foggy feeling in the back of your mind. You will never deal with it until you spell it out in clear words.

Once you do that, look at those guilts and answer this question: "Is it really right for me to feel guilty about this?" You need to be objective, and perhaps someone else may be able to help you take that honest and fair look. Pray about each of those areas of guilt, and ask for God's wisdom as you analyze them. Come to a conclusion about whether or not this guilt is deserved.

Guilt can be either false or true—deserved or undeserved. But it feels the same either way, and we can be easily fooled about what kind it is. Just because you feel guilty doesn't mean you are. Guilt is one of Satan's best weapons—false guilt, that is. And he uses it effectively to debilitate many Christians.

True Guilt

True guilt is what we feel when God is convicting us of some area in our lives that needs to be changed and we are resisting that change. God, however, never intends for us to carry guilt around. He desires that we deal immediately with any conviction that he brings to us, confess it, and permit him to change us. When we are convicted and refuse to take it to God for forgiveness and cleansing, that conviction then turns into guilt. But that isn't from God; rather, it is a result of our failure to deal quickly and decisively with known areas of sin.

If you conclude your guilt is deserved, you will not have any peace until you allow God to deal with it. For instance, if you are experiencing guilt because you have taken a job which is so excessively demanding that you are spending less and less time at home with your children, perhaps God is trying to tell you that he wants you home more often, even if that means changing jobs.

For a couple of years in my career I traveled extensively, probably 35 to 40 percent of the time. My daughter was well cared for, but for me to be away from her that much during her early teens could not have been the best for her. I remember feeling lots of guilt as I rushed to airports week after week, made long distance calls to see how she was doing, and missed important days in her life. I rationalized it away as necessary, but in truth it was not. There were other jobs I could have held that would not have made those demands on me. But I didn't face that guilt; I submerged it and kept doing what I wanted to do.

That is not to say that all working mothers who travel should feel guilty about it. Each of us has differing circumstances. But if you are really willing to face the truth, you should be able to identify those deserved guilts that you are carrying around. When God reveals some of those areas to you, I encourage you not to hesitate in dealing with them. It may appear that the action required is too drastic, too costly. But nothing is more costly in the long term than for a Christian to refuse to deal with known areas of sin or disobedience.

False Guilt

It is my opinion, based on the working mothers I know, that a great part of the guilt these women experience is false guilt. For instance, if you are a single working mother, you're working because it is absolutely essential. The guilt you may feel because you come to work and leave a sick child with the sitter is probably not deserved guilt. The guilt you feel when you cannot be at every school function is another example of false guilt.

And all mothers have learned that kids are very good at laying on false guilt. I think children have inborn instincts at using guilt as a manipulative tool on their parents. Remember, just because your child tells you—either in words or in attitude—that you are the guilty party does not necessarily mean they are right.

Furthermore, working mothers tend to do what divorced parents do—assume that every problem their children have is a result of the fact that they have a working mom or because their parents are divorced. That just is not the case. If you stayed home all the time and devoted every minute of your life to your children, they would still have problems that would baffle you. I recall having lunch with a wonderful young mom who has never worked outside the home. One of her four children was behaving in a most disturbing way. This mother was struggling with what was causing the behavior and how to handle it. But the cause was not that she was a working mom, because she is not.

When you are carrying around false guilt, you need to deal with that just as quickly and decisively as you would true guilt. But of course, you deal with a different source when it is false guilt. Whether the false guilt is from Satan or from your own wrong thinking, it is certain that it is not from God. Therefore, to continue to carry it once you recognize it for what it is, is both foolish and wrong.

Again, we need to pray much about it and ask God to deliver us. Then we have to watch our thought life. That is where false guilt begins. And when that guilt is false, we are not allowed to think about it. Philippians 4:8 gives us our parameters for right thinking, and they are: whatever is true, honorable, right, pure, lovely, of good report, excellent, and worthy of praise. False guilt is not right, it is wrong. Therefore, the guideline is clear: We should not allow ourselves to think those thoughts of false guilt!

The apostle Paul told us that we must take every thought captive to the obedience of Christ (2 Cor. 10:5). It won't happen unless we decide to take those thoughts and, by an act of our will, bring them into line with God's guidelines. In dealing with false guilt, we have to practice this principle over and over again until we destroy that stronghold.

The minute those guilty thoughts start working on your mind, refuse to accept them and replace them with pure, lovely thoughts. If it only lasts five minutes, don't give up. Just replace them again. Depending on how long you've carried that false guilt, it may take a while to break the stronghold it has on your thinking.

Keep another thing in mind as you make decisions about your priorities as a working mom. You have covenant relationships and you have contractual relationships. Covenant relationships are those that you alone can fill. You are the only mother your children have, the only wife of your husband; no one can take your place in your family relationships. These covenant relationships take priority over all others.

Contractual relationships are those where you have some kind of contract, usually a verbal, understood agreement, such as with your employer, the charitable organizations you are a part

of, even your church jobs. True, these are important relationships, but other people could fulfill those roles, and if you walked
out, someone would take your place.

So, as we are faced with priority decisions, it is important to
remember that our covenant relationships are eternal and we
should decide in their favor.

Deciding to Be a Mother

In the last few years, we've seen some real changes in women's
attitudes toward motherhood. Only a short time ago it was rare
indeed for any young girl to even debate whether she would
have children or not. Now, with people marrying much later
and women pursuing new career opportunities, the decision to
not have children is no longer unusual.

I am aware that some Christians believe that it is wrong for
a wife or couple to make that decision. Frankly, I know of no
biblical imperative that would require a wife to have children.
I can see no problem with deciding not to have children, as long
as both husband and wife agree.

However, I think the issue should be carefully and prayer-
fully discussed before marriage. It is not fair to go into a marriage, leading your partner to believe you feel one way about
children and then later on inform him or her that you have
strong feelings about children quite contrary to what he or she
thought. I know couples who have had this happen.

If you are thinking that you might not want children, inves-
tigate your feelings carefully. Be sure they are not simply selfish desires of preserving your freedom or your lifestyle. The
psalmist says that children are a gift from the Lord (Ps. 127:3),
and any couple deciding to not have children should make that
decision very seriously.

The Decision to Continue Working

A more common question faced by young wives is whether
or not to have children and continue to work. I received a let-

ter from a young wife who told me that she wanted to have children soon. But her question to me was, "Is it right for me to have children when I know I'll have to keep working?" Many young wives face this question as they conclude that their second income will continue to be a necessity. And others face it as they realize that they do not want to give up their careers, but they want a family too.

A Christian woman, facing this question, must have one overriding consideration, and that is: "What does God want me to do about this matter?" God has the right to the final word in directing our lives, and since he is a great deal better at it than we are, you can trust him implicitly. Our job is to be willing to obey, even if it does not suit our plans or our ideas. We cannot come to God with preconceived ideas and ask for his okay. We have to come with open hands and hearts and ask to know his plan and be willing to follow it.

It would be simple if there were a specific verse in the Bible that gave direct guidance on whether mothers should work outside their home or not. To my knowledge there is none. But this we know from Scripture: God is very concerned about the family. It is his basic building block for society, and family priorities are very high on his list. With that in mind, let's look at this question of whether it is a good thing for a working woman to have children when she intends to continue working outside the home.

Many successful mothers have worked even when their children were babies. And staying at home with your children is no guarantee that they are going to have a better foundation or be more secure and balanced than other children.

I wish successful parenting could be reduced to a simple formula, such as "If mothers stay home with their children, they can be guaranteed that their children will grow into well-balanced, responsible, productive, delightful young adults." Parenting is the toughest job in the world, and there simply are no guarantees in parenting and no one parental role that works for every child. I don't think anything humbles you more than being a parent, for you realize very early that no matter how good you are or how hard you try, something can go wrong! It really keeps you on your knees.

However, the woman who is thinking of having children and working at the same time needs to be well aware of what she is undertaking. Let me point out a few things, in case you are in that situation.

• *In order to be the mother you want to be and keep a career going, you must be willing to sacrifice.* I think of my sister-in-law, who worked almost continually while raising three children. It was not her first choice to continue working, but since it was necessary, she committed herself to being a first-class mother and maintaining her job as well. Her children are grown now, and she and my brother have every right to be proud of each of them. They are special people, balanced, secure, truly delight-ful young adults, all serving the Lord faithfully. But this did not come without a price to be paid—and the price was paid most heavily by the parents, and by mom, who had to give much more of herself and carry a more difficult schedule than she would have otherwise.

If you asked her, she would tell you that she thoroughly enjoyed being a mother and raising her children. But certainly she had to give a lot more of herself as a dual-role mother, and she had to operate under more pressure and fatigue. She made sure, though, her children never lacked the important things— time with their parents, lots of love and attention, and a sure knowledge that they were the most important things in her life.

Yes, it is possible to be a successful working mom. Absolutely. But before you commit yourself, make sure you understand the job you are undertaking. Read the job description very care-fully. It requires extra sacrifice on your part, especially in those early years when the children demand so much attention.

• *A second consideration is the care of the children while you work.* With all the publicity these days about child abuse in day-care centers, I think working mothers and fathers have a heavy responsibility to insure their children's environment is not only safe but conducive to their growth and maturity. I have to say that a center would have to be exceptional for me to leave my young child there day in and day out. Our church operates an early childhood center in Chicago, and in a center like this, you can rest secure that their care is very good and the environment is Christ-centered. But, of course, not every community has these Christian childcare centers.

When my daughter was small, I had a Christian friend who kept her in her home. That, of course, is a wonderful solution, if it is possible. As Julie got older and was in school, there was a retired Christian couple who came to our home and stayed with her in the afternoons and when I had to travel on business. That way, her routine was not interrupted, and that was a real blessing. In the summers she spent several weeks with my parents in the South, and it was good to know she was under their love and influence for that time.

Of course, not everyone has all these avenues open. You should, therefore, carefully consider how your child will be cared for while you work. It is a crucial decision, and if you are not convinced that you have a suitable plan for that child's care, it should be a critical factor in deciding whether or not to have children and continue to work.

• *A third consideration is to see if you can find a way to earn the needed money without leaving your child.* Many women are creative at doing this. We know that the first six years of a child's life are by far the most crucial. The love and care they receive in those years shape their personality and character for the future. Therefore, being with them, especially during those formative years, is probably your best option. I know that is not always possible, but give it some serious thought. What could you do to earn money at home?

When Julie was little, before I was a single parent, I taught piano in my home. Later I cleaned our church to earn some extra money. That took one or two days a week, and I could take her with me. Now I know that is not an exciting rung on the career ladder, but it kept me with her during those early years. I know women who take care of other children, who sell cosmetics, who do typing and bookkeeping—all from their own homes. Many companies look for what is referred to as cottage help, which means people who will work for them in their homes, doing clerical, telephone, or other work.

By working at home, you cut your expenses dramatically, so it isn't necessary to earn as much money. Without childcare costs—which are high—and clothing and transportation costs, you could probably earn up to 50 percent less at home and still break even. Many times women just look at their salary and think the highest one is best. Don't forget those expenses. Sit down and figure it out. You may be surprised at how much less you can earn if you can stay home and avoid those high expenses.

So, if you are a working woman considering starting your family and continuing to work, sit down and carefully count the cost. If you (or your husband) have the option to stay home during those early years, carefully consider that option. In most situations, you would be well advised to do that. Your child will probably benefit most from having a parent with him or her during those preschool years. Remember, as a Christian mother, God will hold you responsible for the quality of mothering you give your children, much more than how far up the career ladder you climb.

I know working mothers who could stay home, but choose to work because they really don't enjoy the household routine. I understand that mind-set, because I've always felt that I would never be happy with just staying home. I am very active and need lots of things going to keep me from getting bored and lazy. But there are many things we can do while we stay home besides just changing diapers and washing dishes. Any creative woman can include things in her life that meet her own needs for self-improvement and advancement while remaining a stay-at-home mom.

For instance, get involved in a crisis pregnancy center, or start a weekly Bible study for mothers or a child evangelism class for the children in your neighborhood. Do volunteer hospital work, go back to school and finish your degree, go to evening classes to learn new skills, write a book. There are endless things we can do while we stay at home with our children that will give

us the variety and the personal challenge and growth that are
often lacking in the routine work of keeping house.

May I say, parenthetically, that if you think a job will relieve
you of boredom and routine, think again. I have had lots of different kinds of jobs, from clerk to secretary to salesperson to
executive management to owning my own business, and all of
them included routine, boring things that had to be done. Life
is made up of a good number of routine duties, and the happy
person is the one who learns to find meaning and joy in those
routine things.

The Need for a Team Effort

For women who are married, there needs to be a great deal
of understanding and agreement between you and your husband on the sharing of parenting responsibilities as well as household duties. It is best to discuss these things in detail before you
embark on a dual career as a working mother. If you try to be
supermom and carry all the home responsibilities without help
from your husband and family, you will discover quickly that
your effectiveness as a mom, wife, and employee will all suffer.

The best way to do this without ongoing conflict is to establish with your husband how various duties will be shared, with
a firm agreement from him to be responsible for certain things
on an ongoing basis. And as the children are old enough, they
need assignments of their own to share the housework.

My career has been as a single working mom, so I have never
personally faced the challenge of working out these details. But
I know many couples who have found that satisfactory middle
ground where they share duties willingly on a predetermined
basis. It works best when you openly and frequently discuss the
team effort that is needed.

Also, it is important that parenting responsibilities be shared.
(Of course, that is true whether you are a working mom or not.)
You need to discuss issues such as the way you will deal with
sick children and who will stay with them. And as your children

age, there will be school responsibilities and commitments that need to be shared, as well as chauffeuring and other involvement in the activities of your children.

The more these things are ironed out ahead of time, the better chance you will have for a successful team effort as workplace parents. When you fail to agree on these issues, the consequences for all can be very destructive. If you feel your husband is not carrying his share of the responsibilities, you are likely to harbor anger and resentment, which can turn into arguments and can result in a damaged relationship. And of course, your child will sense the tension and struggle between the two of you, which will have detrimental effects on the child.

Being a workplace mom can place additional stress on your relationship with your husband, and will require better communication and more effort on the part of both of you to make certain that you work as a team.

Priorities—Again!

It is so easy for us to focus on things that are not important to God. A working mother really has a balancing act to perform, and it is critical that she have a good understanding of what the priorities are.

I look back on my years as a working mother and sadly recognize that many times my career took precedence over my role as mother. I really botched it badly at times. If I had it to do over, I'd do some things differently—probably turn down some jobs that I took and not worry so much about earning more money or buying a nicer home or proving to the world how successful I could be as a career woman.

Is my daughter ruined? No, in his great mercy, God has covered for many of my errors and turned my ashes into beauty again. But undoubtedly Julie has missed some mothering that she needed. I cannot go back and fill in the missing blanks. God can do that for her, as she learns to trust him, and he can use it for her good. I believe that strongly, and therefore I don't live in fear or guilt over my mistaken priorities. But both of us have missed some things we should have experienced because of my misplaced priorities at times.

Of course, every mother in the world will tell you that you always wish you could go back and correct your mistakes. There's no way to do it perfectly as a parent. God does not need perfect parents, but he needs mothers and fathers who put him first in their lives, and then put their families first in their priorities.

Let me reemphasize that parenting is a difficult task, though one of the most wonderful experiences in all of life. Being a successful mother does not depend on whether you work outside the home or not. I want to encourage the working mothers reading this, especially those who have no choice, that you can be the mother God wants you to be, and your children can have the attention and nurturing they need. You and your children are not doomed for failure just because you work.

There is a price to pay, and for working moms it is giving a lot of yourself, of your time and energy. Time that you might prefer to spend quietly reading, time when you would like to go to bed early, or time when you really didn't want to go to a school function after working all day. These are the sacrifices that are very real for working moms.

The most important thing you can do is pour prayer time into this situation. A praying mom, one whose life is absolutely on track with the Lord, who spends time in his Word, and lives it before her children is what your children need. You can be that kind of mom, whether you work outside your home or not.

I am well aware that there are many different opinions on this subject, especially within the Christian community. I'm quite certain that many wonderful Christians would disagree with some of my opinions in this chapter on working moms. If you start asking advice, you'll probably get a different view from almost everyone you ask.

God's Leading

It is a great comfort to know that God does not lead us all exactly the same way. You need to know what God would have you do, and the marvelous thing is that he wants you to know that. If you will pray for his wisdom, and be willing to obey whatever it is, he will give his guidance to you personally. I am not the final word on this subject, and neither is any other person. But God is quite capable, and most willing, to impart to you his plan for you, if you are just willing to listen and obey.

Back to basics again—spend much time getting to know God. Learn how to hear his voice and distinguish it from all others. That comes through time in his Word and in prayer, quality and quantity time. Keep that priority first, and you can be assured of his personal guidance for you as a working mother.

12

Job Hunting
and Unemployment

Like most of you, I've gone through the job hunting routine more than once, with résumés and interviews and acceptances and rejections. Some of those job searches have been desperate, some have been volitional, others have been a shopping expedition to see what was out there in moments of boredom or curiosity. Regardless, they all are exhausting, traumatic, and tense.

At one point or another, most people in the working world begin to look around the job market to see if they can find a job they like better or one that pays more money. In fact, some people do it on a continual basis. However, job hunting is a particularly difficult time when you're under pressure to find a new job, whether as a result of being laid off or fired, or entering the job market for the first time or reentering it after a period of absence. A pressurized job hunt can come about, too, when your current job is extremely disagreeable or the environment is particularly detrimental to your emotional, physical, or mental well-being.

It's that kind of pressurized job hunting that I want to address in this chapter. If you're not in that particular situation at the moment, I urge you to keep reading anyway. In the economic environment of the '90s, many who never dreamed they would ever be in a desperate job hunt are finding themselves there, and many more are anticipating it. This decade is a downsizing, fat-cutting period for American business, and the job climate is changing in dramatic ways. Few people will work for one company their whole career anymore, and most will change jobs several times during their working life. It's a fact many of us are facing with trepidation, but the reality is there.

Job hunting pressure very soon and very easily turns into anxiety, worry, and fear! These are the chief enemies of job hunters under pressure. If that's how you feel, then you're quite normal.

Let me ask you a question: Does it make any difference, at these times, that you're a Christian? It's so easy to quip a yes answer to that question, when things are going fine. But when you get up in the morning under pressure to find a job, and there is that knot in your stomach, and you say "What do I do today? I must find a job. What will happen if I don't find a job soon? Will anyone ever give me a chance?"—does it make any difference then that you are a Christian?

Most of us, like children, long for easy ways out. And when it's not easy, we cry and complain. Those are normal human reactions. But Jesus came to give us the power to be more than normal! We don't have to be held captive by our normal human tendencies. Because of Jesus Christ, we can be absolutely joyful and peaceful in the midst of pressurized job hunting. That is victorious living, and if you're not experiencing it as a Christian, then Satan, your enemy, is robbing you of what is rightfully yours.

Just this very day, as I write this, I have answered a letter from a woman under great pressure—a single mom who needs a job and can't find one. I could feel her terror as I read her letter, and I tried to give her some practical advice about job hunting as well as some encouragement and understanding as to why she is in this terrible spot. When we find ourselves in these difficult kinds of situations, especially when it is not of our doing and we don't deserve it, the first thing most of us ask is "Why me?" That's okay; go ahead and ask it.

Why is God allowing you to go through this period of uncertainty and frustration? Why are you having to experience this seemingly debilitating and humiliating experience of being unemployed and looking for a job? If God is God, and if he really loves you as he says he does, why wouldn't he just land that perfect job in your lap and deliver you from all this torture? What possible good could come from this experience of job hunting under pressure?

Learning to Trust God

The most important thing to God is for us to learn how to trust him. Could it be that this is the one sure way God could get your attention and thereby teach you to rely on him? If you can truly trust him when you're out of work, at a time when you would normally be ravaged with anxiety and fear, when the future is unknown to you, then you know you're learning to trust. Could it be that you were looking to your job for security instead of to the Lord? Maybe he had to knock those props out from under you in order to make it possible for you to learn how to put your confidence in him.

One of my dearest friends has held the same, dependable job for twenty-three years. Yet there are now rumors the company may be sold, and what she thought was a lifetime job with great security could be swept away at any time. She told me, "I had no idea how much I looked to my job for security until this happened. I'm learning what it means to really trust God in ways I've never learned before."

Mind you, this comes from one of the most spiritually-minded women I know who loves and serves the Lord with all her being. But this new predicament of facing the possibility of being unemployed is driving her into new depths of trust, revealing areas of fear and unbelief in her heart that she never knew were there.

Without these tight spots in our lives we would have no opportunity to find out experientially that God's promises are true and that he is truly capable of meeting all our needs. And God, who has a long-term perspective and knows that in the end he is going to take care of us and meet all our needs, allows these times as a way for us to learn to trust him in new depth. Without faith it's impossible to please God, and we must learn to be thankful for any situation that strengthens and increases our faith, because that makes us more pleasing to our heavenly Father.

Slowly, I'm beginning to come to the place where I can truly thank God for tough, unpleasant, impossible situations—situations where my hands are tied, my options are gone, my efforts have failed, and my own ingenuity is ineffective. Gradually my earthbound mind is accepting the principle that it is only when everything looks hopeless and bleak that I can move into a new understanding of God and develop a deeper confidence in him.

When I can focus my mind on that truth, and when I can view my circumstances from an eternal perspective, then I can honestly say from my heart that I'm glad to have the opportunity to learn to know my God in ways I never would have otherwise.

But I want to tell you that it is not easy, it is not once and for all. It takes discipline, a consistent devotional life, and a continual regrouping of my thoughts. When I say that I am just beginning to learn this, that is exactly what I mean. Learning is, after all, repetition. We learn to do things as we repeatedly try and fail, and try again.

So don't be discouraged when you find you must keep trying, keep starting all over again. Failure is not defeat. In this process of learning to be truly thankful for the unknown, uncontrollable, difficult circumstances of my life, I'm quite certain that my failures have exceeded my successes. But I just refuse to quit because down underneath all the fears and apprehensions that keep raising their ugly heads I really do want to know God in new ways. Sometimes I can even feel excited about the prospects as I envision the joy and freedom of learning to trust God when there is no sight, no tangible reality, no human hope.

If it weren't hard, I could figure it out for myself and just go merrily along. But when it is beyond me, when it is too hard for me, then I can have the great privilege of asking and allowing God to intervene and watching him change me and the situation.

Looking for Security

Have you been looking to your job for your security? Do you think of your job as your means of support? I have a Christian friend who used to work with me, and she would always say, "This company is not my source." I often think of Ruby and remember that affirmation of faith she taught me in a real way. No company can be my source of security or meet my needs. Depending on a job, no matter how good it is, is dangerous ground.

When we can start looking to God as our security, and recognizing that we are his responsibility and not dependent on anyone but him for our future, then we begin to know real freedom. Ruby was laid off by that company we both worked for. It certainly was not a pleasant experience for her, but her faith never budged. Not because she was independently wealthy or was just working for the fun of it! No, she was not worried about being laid off because she had not placed her confidence in that job or that company and being without it was not a disaster to her. She simply expected God, who knew her needs, to give her something better.

I am self-employed, which means I do not have a salary coming in every month. My income is not guaranteed. It's been that way for about ten years now, and from time to time I still struggle with the fear of not having any money to pay the bills. But I can see how God has used this situation, this lack of security in an employer, to teach me to trust him so much more.

Putting your faith in God really sets you free from worry about what's going to happen to you. That may sound terribly basic, but few Christians ever get to that place in their walk with God. It is absolutely incredible how many of us continue to carry our own burdens and shoulder all the responsibility for ourselves. We won't allow God to be God in our lives and to do for us what he is so totally capable and willing to do because we just will not trust him.

If indeed your current predicament of unemployment is the way you will learn to trust Jesus more fully than ever before, can't you agree that it is a good thing for you?

The Sin of Unbelief

God continues to show me how he despises unbelief in my life. Not depending on God to do what he has promised is a serious thing. It's not just that we don't have enough faith. It is, rather, that we refuse to trust. That's what strikes me as I read the third chapter of Hebrews. The people of Israel refused to trust God, not because they didn't have enough faith or they weren't spiritual enough or they didn't know enough about God. No, they refused to trust God because of the wickedness of their heart.

That's a pretty serious indictment, don't you agree? For me, the lack of trust in my life is taking on a new dimension. I no longer can excuse myself or treat it lightly, for I'm beginning to realize that God doesn't treat it lightly. Not believing him indicates that there is wickedness in my heart.

And if I can indeed refuse to rely on him, then it means that I can do just the opposite also, and that is, make a decision to rely on him—or in other words, refuse *not* to trust him. Trusting God does not depend upon my level of faith or my stage of spiritual growth. It depends on the set of my will, and no matter who you are or what your predicament is, you have the ability to decide to trust God. That is a choice you make.

If you're not yet depending on God in this situation of unemployment—or any other situation for that matter—will you just stop right now and realize that the reason you are not trusting is that there is within you an evil heart of unbelief. I don't mean to sound harsh, but I truly do believe that that is how God views our lack of trust. And if that is how he sees it, we really need to take this more seriously than we have in the past.

Now, I want to encourage you that this is not a onetime thing. You must set your will to trust him, and then determine that every time the doubts and fears come, you will, by a set of your will, against all your emotions, stop and tell yourself and God that you choose to trust him. Don't be stubborn like the people of Israel who hardened their hearts, but be willing to turn your will over to him—many times.

A friend was telling me that she is highly susceptible to a fear about whether or not she can perform her new job adequately. She knows that fear is of Satan, and she knows this is a satanic attack on her to try to destroy her confidence and her trust in God. She knows that through Christ she can overcome that fear. But even with that knowledge, she must continually remind herself every time that fear raises its ugly head that she has freedom from that fear through Christ. She has to stop and again set her will to trust God.

So don't be surprised when this happens to you. It is true with all of us who are daily walking with the Lord as a lifestyle. Lessons God taught me in a dramatic way months or years ago I have to reapply almost daily. But each time I do, my faith is increased and my commitment is strengthened. And Satan's stronghold in my life is loosened each time I decide to put my confidence in God, rather than to give way to my fears and anxiety.

Becoming an Encourager

Perhaps God wants to teach you compassion so that you can be understanding and helpful to others who experience a similar difficulty. Second Corinthians 1:5–7 (PHILLIPS) says:

> Indeed, experience shows that the more we share Christ's immeasurable suffering the more we are able to give of his encouragement. This means that if we experience trouble it is for your comfort and spiritual protection; for if we ourselves have been comforted we know how to encourage you to endure patiently the same sort of troubles that we ourselves endure. We are quite confident that if you have to suffer troubles as we have done, then, like us, you will find the comfort and encouragement of God.

If someone says to you, "You know, I was unemployed like you once, and I well remember how frightened and insecure I was," don't you tend to give more credibility to what that person has to say? They can really minister to you in your need. We need encouragers so much in the body of Christ today. Maybe God is preparing you to be an encourager.

You can be sure that God has a purpose for taking you through this time of uncertainty and frustration. Now, can you be thankful that he is willing to take the time and effort to shape you into who he wants you to be? Can you thank him for taking you through this experience so that you can become more effective for him? In James 1:2–4 (PHILLIPS) we read:

> When all kinds of trials and temptations crowd into your lives, my brothers, don't resent them as intruders, but welcome them as friends! Realise that they come to test your faith and to produce in you the quality of endurance. But let the process go on until that endurance is fully developed, and you will find you have become men of mature character, men of integrity with no weak spots.

Can you truly welcome this period of unemployment and this time of pressurized job hunting as a friend rather than an intruder? Will you believe that as a result you are going to emerge from this experience with a steadfastness that you did not have before, and that therefore you will be more like Jesus Christ and more usable in his service? If that then is the case, isn't it worthwhile?

Let me, in closing, just remind you of some wonderful passages of comfort and strength:

> They who seek the LORD shall not be in want of any good thing.
> Psalm 34:10

> Don't worry over anything whatever; whenever you pray tell God every detail of your needs in thankful prayer, and the peace of God, which surpasses human understanding, will keep constant guard over your hearts and minds as they rest in Christ Jesus.
> Philippians 4:6 PHILLIPS

> My God shall supply all your needs according to His riches in glory in Christ Jesus.
> Philippians 4:19

Delight yourself in the LORD;
And He will give you the desires of your heart.
                                            Psalm 37:4

If you are a child of God, these promises are for you. You can claim them right in the middle of the unemployment you are experiencing. And you can prove in your life that they are really true.

13

Covering
Our Corner
of the World

Before he departed into heaven, Jesus told his disciples: "You shall be My witnesses both in Jerusalem, and in all Judea and Samaria, and even to the remotest part of the earth" (Acts 1:8).

Earlier we said that although we cannot preach or teach or continually witness, our lives can become that inescapable witness to what God can do for and with any person who is committed to him. And we have talked a lot about how our behavior in handling many problems on the job can lead our colleagues to wonder and eventually to ask what makes us different. But now let's consider witnessing in a more active sense.

What meaning does it have for us today to be witnesses in Jerusalem and Judea and Samaria? Well, when we look at a map, we see that Jesus was in Jerusalem, and Judea was the territory surrounding Jerusalem, and Samaria was farther away than Judea. So, Jesus is giving us a principle, that we witness first of all right where we are—whatever our Jerusalem is. And then we are responsible to let that witness grow and include the remotest part of the earth.

Most Christians are willing to witness to the remote parts of the earth by supporting missionaries, for example, but they won't tackle witnessing in their Jerusalem. That's truly getting the cart before the horse. Jesus said to start in our corner of the world, and for us working people, that has to include our jobs. It's a clear command from Jesus, and that elevates this issue to highest importance. Jesus said that if we love him, we will keep his commandments, and he has commanded us to be witnesses right where we live and work.

Hindrances to Effective Witnessing

A friend once said to me, "You know, I don't really witness on my job. I know I should, but I don't. The problem is I have to go back the next day and face those people." I surely can relate to how she feels, can't you?

I think the hardest place to be a witness is on our jobs, because we see these people every day. They know us at our best—and at our worst. When you're with someone on a day-in, day-out basis, you can't cover up. They know the real you. And I think one of the reasons we hesitate to witness is that we fear they will not accept our witness, since they know, and we know they know, that we're not perfect.

Furthermore, we tend to view our work environments as inappropriate places to witness. It's much easier to share the gospel where the environment is conducive, and we don't feel very spiritually minded at work. Since spiritual subjects are rarely discussed in work environments, our doing so might categorize us as different or strange. And, let's face it, none of us want to be rejected.

Also, we haven't had many role models to show us or inspire us in this matter of witnessing on the job; and when we do have an opportunity to verbally share our faith in some way, many of us are uneducated. We often don't know the best way to share with unbelievers because of lack of practice or study.

All of these reasons and others as well combine to make us tongue-tied and fearful of giving a clear-cut witness on our jobs.

Sad to say, there are many Christians whose coworkers would never guess that they are Christians. I know that has been true of me at times in my career.

Preliminaries to Effective Witnessing

How can we overcome these hindrances and become lights in the part of the world to which we are sent? It begins with that changed attitude we have spoken of. If we desire to be an effective witness, we cannot, consciously or subconsciously, see ourselves as part-time Christians, fitting our commitment to Christ around our jobs and other responsibilities. We cannot treat our jobs as separate parts of our lives—secular rather than sacred.

Second, in order to have an effective witness, our lives must be clean before God. That doesn't mean we have to be perfect; it doesn't mean that because we've blown it at work before, no one will believe us. Satan tries to tell us that any past failure ruins our chances to witness. But that is a lie. God is in the business of turning our ashes into beauty, of taking our weaknesses and making us strong through them. You don't have to have an unblemished, perfect record in order to witness. But your life must be clean. If there is known sin, known rebellion of any kind on your part, your witness will be hindered.

While most of us have difficulty sharing our faith, there are some people who can be almost too verbal about their faith, especially if their talk doesn't match their walk. In fact, some of you may find yourself in the uncomfortable situation of having a believer as a coworker who is very verbal, but whose life is a poor testimony. That is a most difficult spot to be in.

Third, before a witness can be effective, there have to be listening ears. Jesus frequently said, "He that hath ears to hear, let him hear." That simply means that not everyone wants to hear, and without a desire to hear, a person will not hear. Of course, we don't always know who those people are. But we must be careful not to verbally assault anyone with the gospel; we need to sense an opening and a desire, no matter how small, to hear.

Jesus said, "Do not throw your pearls before swine" (Matt. 7:6). He certainly didn't mean that he considered people to be swine. It's just that we should not take something so precious to us as our experience with the Lord and throw it in front of someone who has no sensitivity for the beauty of that pearl. Pigs have extremely poor eyesight and can't distinguish things of value.

To people in darkness, your pearl is indistinguishable from all the other garbage that is thrown in front of them. They get their kicks from drinking all night; you get yours from religion. That's frequently how they view it. And until there is some receptivity on their part, be careful not to throw what you value before those with no capacity to receive it.

I can think of a person in my life presently to whom I want to witness. I've made many attempts, but I can sense that the ears are just not open. This person is not the least interested in finding answers right now. But I'm hanging in there, ready to talk when it's appropriate, saying whatever I can when I can, maintaining the friendship so that if there is ever an open heart, I'll be there, ready to witness.

I can also think of a particular occasion when I threw pearls before swine. A past business associate and friend was in town and wanted to get together for dinner. I remember that I had a heavy schedule that week and had reserved that evening to study and prepare for an upcoming speaking engagement. Yet I felt it would be selfish of me to refuse the invitation, because I might have an opportunity to share Jesus with this friend.

As the evening wore on, it was impossible for me to turn the conversation to anything spiritual. My friend had a few drinks and was in no mood whatsoever to hear about my relationship with Jesus or what Jesus could do in her life. Instead, I had to listen to conversation about totally insignificant things, and when I did force a word or two of witness in edgewise, it was treated with disdain and condescension.

Though my motives were good, my discernment was poor. I had thrown my precious pearl before swine, and it just felt terrible. I wanted to yell, "Don't you understand, this is the most important thing in the whole world. Listen to me!" But I forgot that she had no way at this point of understanding the great value of my pearl.

When I finally got home, I said, "Lord, where did I fail? I wanted to share you with my friend. But it was just a terrible evening, and I wasted all that time, which puts me very much behind schedule now. What did I do wrong?" A couple of days later, as I was reading this passage in Matthew 6, God quietly explained it to me. I had a clear object lesson of what it means to throw pearls before swine. I discovered that I have to develop discernment for open ears that are ready to hear.

Creating a Desire to Hear

Think with me: What does it take to create a desire to hear and know about God? What is the essential ingredient? It takes the Word of God—right? Romans 10:17 tells us that "faith comes from hearing, and hearing by the word of Christ." But how can we speak the Word to someone who has no desire to hear it? If it takes the Word of God to create a desire for someone to hear it, how do we get the Word of God to them in order to create the desire?

Did you know that there's more than one edition of the Word of God? The written Word of God, which we call the Scriptures, is not the only way to communicate God's message. Listen to what Paul wrote in 2 Corinthians 3:2–3:

> You are our letter, written in our hearts, known and read by all men; being manifested that you are a letter of Christ, cared for by us, written not with ink, but with the Spirit of the living God, not on tablets of stone, but on tablets of human hearts.

The second edition of the Bible is this living Word that Paul writes about. When we live the Word of God before people, they cannot ignore it or dismiss it. And eventually when they see the Word of God in our lives, they're going to want to know more about it.

For instance, suppose you get to work next week and discover that the place is in an uproar. Maybe you're a nurse, and every other nurse on your floor is angry at the head nurse. They're all griping and complaining, upset beyond words. Perhaps they even have a right to be upset. And, of course, they expect you to be upset with them and to join in with their complaining and condemnation of the head nurse.

But suppose, without a word, you simply keep your cool, refuse to be drawn into the discontent, and remain peaceful and undisturbed. If you continue to abide in Christ in the midst of all that conflict, you've become a living Word. Your coworkers have just been forced to read the Word of God. They read Ephesians, or several psalms, right there in front of their eyes. It comes in a form they cannot tune out or dismiss. And when the Word goes forth it always accomplishes that to which it was sent. So that Word they see in you begins to take root.

If you consistently live the Word of God, eventually someone will be curious, and will ask you something like, "How can you be the way you are? How can you stay so cool in the midst of this dog-eat-dog environment?" They're asking you for answers! Wow, this is what you've been waiting for. First Peter 3:15 tells us to "always [be] ready to make a defense to everyone who asks you to give an account for the hope that is in you, yet with gentleness and reverence." Now, it's your responsibility to be ready for an answer. No faltering here; no hemming and hawing around; no hesitation. You have open ears before you, and now you give the verbal Word of God with clarity and love and gentleness.

Since I wrote the first of edition of this book, I have acquired a wonderful new friend who came to know me through it. She was given the book when graduating from law school and decided to look me up. Her name is Janet, and she is a wonderful Christian working woman, whom I admire and love greatly.

Her story of finding Christ illustrates this so well. Before getting her law degree, she earned a Ph.D. in immunology. She worked as a scientist in a hectic lab environment, where everyone was under constant pressure, working long hours, and feeling stressed out all the time. In the midst of this difficult situation, she noticed one coworker, Jim, who never seemed to be stressed out. Yet he was as smart and worked as hard as everyone else. She kept watching him.

Finally, one day she said to him, "Jim, I've been watching you. How can you stay calm when the rest of us are going bonkers?" There's that question Peter was talking about, and Jim was ready. Quietly, he told Janet that the only thing he could think of was because he was a Christian. Well, Janet figured she was too, but Jim got her attention and she started talking to him about being a Christian. He urged her to read the Book of John. She had never read the Bible before, so she decided to do so.

Night after night she read the Gospels, and during the day she would often talk to Jim about it. Gradually, she fell in love with the Jesus she was getting to know, and one night by herself, she knelt and asked Jesus to come into her life. A few months later her husband did the same thing. And now, eight or so years later, they are vibrant testimonies in their workplaces, lights in the darkness.

And all because one Christian was the living Word of God, and his life made Janet thirsty for that living Water. Jim had the joy of quietly sharing Jesus with Janet. Now, let me tell you, it is exciting when you see God do something like that through you. If you've never experienced that thrill, you've missed something really terrific.

Each situation is different. We can say a lot to some people; others only allow us a few sentences here and there. But we must be looking for these opportunities to tell about the hope that is in us. While it's true that some Christians witness insensitively and do harm in that way, it is far more often the case that we Christians don't use the opportunities we have. We are asked questions, in one form or another, that give us open doors, and we aren't prepared or willing to take our stand and give a strong witness.

Our Ultimate Role Model for Witnessing

Notice how Jesus witnessed to people. Sometimes he just dropped a statement that left everyone curious. People were always asking, "What manner of man is this?" There is example after example in Scripture of Jesus' method of witnessing, and it was always to create a desire and a curiosity on the part of the listener. Jesus asks the Samaritan woman for a drink of water. He didn't walk up to her and say, "Woman, I am the promised Messiah. Believe on me and be saved." What do you think she would have done if he had? Probably thought he was crazy and gotten out of there as soon as possible. Instead, he created a curiosity and desire in her to know who he was. He did not defend himself against her charges. He ignored those accusing remarks she made. He kept looking for a way to make her want to know who he was. He continued to talk about living water. And then she said, "Sir, give me this water."

She asked him for something. She didn't even fully understand it yet, but she wanted what he had.

That's our perfect model for witnessing. Create a desire by living the Word of God in front of your coworkers daily. If you display the fruits of the Spirit of God in your life consistently, you will be noticed. It will be different from what is expected, and you'll have opportunities to give an answer as to why you're different.

Missionaries to the Working World

If you, like me, have spent any time in an evangelical church, you have undoubtedly heard missionaries home on furlough testifying to what God is doing through them in their places of service. I can recall many stories of missionaries who spent years in a faraway land, tirelessly translating Scripture and learning the culture of those unreached people, waiting years for an opportunity to be able to clearly give them the gospel. They tell how they became servants to these people, nursing them, teaching them, and building strong relationships with them in order to gain their confidence and earn the right to tell them God's Good News.

We hear those accounts, and our eyes fill with tears and our hearts stir within us as we thank God for their dedication, patience, and sacrificial love. And mentally, we put those missionaries in a special category of people (though they never want us to do that), thinking of them as especially gifted and used of God to reach those poor dying souls who have never before heard the gospel.

Are those souls in faraway lands more precious to God than the souls of the people with whom we work? No, of course not, because God is no respecter of persons (Acts 10:34). Well then, who is going to reach those people you work with? Does it not make sense that you have been put there as a witness, just as surely as the missionary was sent to unreached people?

If our avenue of reaching them is to create a desire on their part, as they watch our lives, then our lives are going to have to be different, unique. We will have to become servants, too, just as the missionaries do. Our serving will take different forms. Maybe it is helping someone else with a project and not receiving credit for it. Maybe it is enduring unfair treatment without complaining. Maybe it is refusing to defend ourselves when we are falsely accused, or purposing in our hearts to love people we don't like.

Whatever our particular circumstances, we cannot view our jobs as others view their jobs if indeed we want to be a missionary to that corner of the world. Instead of fighting for our rights, instead of complaining when the work is piled on, instead of looking for ways to cut corners, we look for ways to become servants, ways to let the love of God show through us. Because we know when that happens, we will create a desire on the part of others to know what makes us different, and then they'll start asking us questions. And we can do what we're really there to do—tell them God's Good News.

If missionaries are called to do that in lands across the sea, we are just as surely called to do that in our working worlds. If missionaries are responsible to witness to the people in their worlds, we are equally responsible to witness to those in ours. It is no easier for missionaries to become servants and give up their rights than it is for us. They are not given some special anointing that is denied to us. The power to do it is ours through the Holy Spirit. The command to do it is absolutely clear from our Savior.

When we stand before the judgment seat of Christ, shoulder to shoulder with missionaries and others who were in public ministries, do you really believe God is going to use a different yardstick for us than he does for them? If they are to die to themselves, so are we. If they are to sacrifice money, career, family, and so forth, for the sake of the gospel, so are we.

If we could just get this concept through to our hearts, and really change the way we view our jobs, we could win so many more people in our corners of the world.

Isn't it apparent why God puts us in these environments with non-Christians? While most of those people might never read the Bible or hear it preached, with you there in the midst of them as an example of the living Word, they cannot avoid reading you. And that will create a hunger and thirst on the part of some of them.

Remember, Jesus taught us that many people will not receive the Word. He told us that the gate is straight and the road is narrow that leads to life, and few find it. So don't be surprised when not everyone is interested. However, don't fail to give the Word whenever you can, even when it looks hopeless, because we can never tell what is in that heart. What looks like tough, hard soil to us may be fertile, rich soil underneath. Our job is to plant the seed. We are not responsible for the outcome.

Using Failure as a Witness

I want to encourage you to set your mind toward becoming a witness. And I want to encourage you not to let past failure keep you from starting again. Don't let the fact that you haven't always been a perfect testimony keep you from becoming a witness for him. None of us could ever be witnesses if that were true.

You know, you are not the only person in the world who fails. Isn't that good news! Learning to live and deal with failure is the subject of many books. Obviously, all of us deal with some degree of failure; so, the fact that you have failed to be the perfect Christian example at all times is not an acceptable excuse for refusing to witness. I think many Christians fall into this failure syndrome and almost view it as real humility. Allowing past failure to keep us from witnessing is not an evidence of humility for a Christian. It is rather an evidence that there is lack of trust in God's power to forgive and restore.

Whatever your failures have been, if you've confessed them to God and received his forgiveness, you can still be an effective witness for the Lord. In fact, God could even use your failures as a witness.

Let me give you an example. I remember one particular time when my behavior in front of one of my peers was anything but gentle, loving, kind, patient, long-suffering, or humble. Something had irritated me, and all those fruits of the Spirit of God that I should have been wearing just fell right off. (Undoubtedly, it happened more than once, but this book isn't large enough to list all of them!) I had been encouraging a colleague in things of the Lord, sharing my relationship with the Lord, helping him to begin a serious devotional life. And after all those spiritual discussions, I behaved in just the opposite manner.

When I got home that evening, God's Spirit really convicted me and I was truly embarrassed to realize how badly I had blown it. My first thought was that my friend would now discount everything I had said before, that all that spiritual progress he had made would be lost because I failed so badly as a Christian, right before his eyes.

But the faithful Spirit of God showed me what I had to do. The next morning, as soon as I could, I got alone with my friend and apologized. I told him exactly how I felt, how convicted I was, and how sorry I was that I had failed. But then I went on to explain how wonderful it is that even when we fail so miserably, God's forgiveness and his healing are always available.

Though I would have much preferred that the incident had never occurred, God in his great mercy and efficiency used my failure to show this person another beautiful attribute of our Lord and Savior. He had an object lesson in forgiveness right in front of his eyes. Our conversation revealed that failure and the fear of failure were real problems with this person. So, my failure became an avenue of witness to the wonderful forgiveness and acceptance Jesus offers to his disciples.

Once at my weekly small group Bible study, one of the girls admitted that, without thinking, she had lied to her manager that morning. She was feeling bad about it. We all could relate to her, because we all can remember times when we've done the same thing. "What do I do?" she asked. Our advice was to go right in the next morning, tell her boss exactly what had happened, apologize for the lie, and get it settled. And we pointed out how God could use even that failure—that sin—to speak to that boss. It could offer her a wonderful opportunity to explain why that lie bothered her so much—and why, though no harm was done, she could not allow it to be left that way.

Don't you imagine that her boss has lied before? Who knows, maybe she was right then struggling with a sense of failure and longing to know forgiveness and peace. Don't you imagine that her boss has had many employees lie to her before? But how many ever came back and admitted it and asked for forgiveness? Failure can be used by God to bring a witness to his wonderful forgiveness that is available to everyone.

A Full-Time Commitment

I trust, as a Christian in the working world, that you have a proper perspective of your job and that you view yourself as a Christian committed to full-time service to your Lord. He is worthy of every ounce we can ever give, and nothing else is of eternal significance.

I hope and pray you have caught the vision of what could happen if every Christian in the working world became a full-time Christian, using his or her job primarily as an opportunity to share Christ in that corner of the world, in that Jerusalem. The potential is staggering. The command of our Lord is unequivocal and clear. The field is ripe unto harvest. And, oh, how our friends and associates in our business worlds need the message we can give them.